MW01250468

Decision Making and the Role of
Ash-Shura in Saudi Arabia

*This book belongs to
Leila F. Dane*

Decision Making and the Role of *Ash-Shura* in Saudi Arabia

Majlis Ash-Shura (Consultative Council):
Concept, Theory and Practice

Faisal bin Mishaal bin Saud Al-Saud, Ph.D.

Foreword by Nelson Mandela

VANTAGE PRESS
New York   2003

The opinions expressed herein are solely those of the author.

FIRST EDITION

All rights reserved, including the right of
reproduction in whole or in part in any form.

Copyright © 2003, 2004 by Faisal bin Mishaal bin Saud Al-Saud, Ph.D.

Published by Vantage Press, Inc.
419 Park Ave. South, New York, NY 10016

This book was originally published with the title *Islamic Political Development in the Kingdom of Saudi Arabia: Majlis Ash-Shura: Concept, Theory and Practice.* After careful considerations the title was changed to be more suitable to the contents of the book.

Manufactured in the United States of America
ISBN: 0-533-14678-X

Library of Congress Catalog Card No.: 2003094571

0 9 8 7 6 5 4 3 2 1

Contents

GLOSSARY

A'kida	:	Creed
Al Sunna	:	The traditions of the Prophet.
Ash – Shura	:	Consultation or taking counsel from the knowledgeable and wise in both spiritual and material sciences.
Bida'	:	An innovation or novelty (the opposite of Sunna)
Fikh	:	The name given to jurisprudence in Islam.
Faqih	:	Jurisprudence in Islam.
Fatwa	:	A formal legal opinion given by a mufti.
Mufti	:	A person in a legal authority to give formal legal opinions.
Majlis Ash-Shura	:	Consultative council in Islam. It is similar to parliaments or legislative bodies in Western political systems.
Hadith	:	The sayings of the Prophet.
Imam	:	Prayer leader or a leader of a Muslim nation.
Kurān	:	The Book of Islam containing the words spoken by God delivered to Prophet Muhammad (Pbuh).
Shari'a	:	The body of formally established sacred laws in Islam.
U'lama	:	Scholars who are trained in the religious studies.
Wahhabiya	:	An Islamic community founded in Central Arabia by Muhammad Ibn Abd – al Wahhab.
Umma	:	Nation or community of believers.
Ijtihad	:	To exert an effort in interpreting and deliberating Islamic Law (s).

Transliteration

The system of transliteration which is applied in this
book is that of the Encyclopedia of Islam.

Foreword

We once spoke of the world as a global village wishfully, anticipating a time when human solidarity and friendship will transcend national boundaries and other divides. The new globalized world order unfortunately does not, in the first place, express such solidarity and friendship. It is based rather on the accessibility of markets and the free flow of trade, money and goods. This global village often serves to the advantage of some and to the detriment of others, which is the antithesis of global friendship.

Amidst all of that, though, there has been a flowering of relationships and friendship, facilitated by the ease of communication and contact in the modern world. It is a great privilege to contribute in this way to a book on a country that we as South Africans, and I personally, can proudly count as a friend.

That the book is written by one who is a personal friend adds enormously to that privilege and honor. We intend our humble contribution as a tribute to friendship and solidarity.

The book itself is a proud reminder of the wealth of local and regional histories, cultures and polities that constitute the contemporary globalized world. This book records important socio-political developments in Saudi Arabia and is written by a person with a deep personal knowledge of developments in that country and the broader region.

I am always deeply struck by social and economic developments in countries with political systems that may differ from those that we are used to in Western democracies. Saudi Arabia, for example, has built a modern economy over a short period of time. This has produced significant advantages for the local population. Education, health and other social services are available to many more people, economic opportunities abound, life expectancy has risen and the general quality of life is high.

All of this has been achieved in the period in which the world has shrunk considerably. Developments in one part of the world are swiftly known in another. Comparisons are inevitably drawn between countries where, in the past, it might have been readily accepted that countries are different and will develop along different trajectories.

It is this reduction of distances that has tended to impose on the entire world a uniform view on democracy. The tendency has increasingly been to view democracy as the set of institutions and cultural assumptions that are prevalent in the West. This view of democracy has always run into problems because the world is a culturally diverse place and no single culture has the monopoly on democratic practice. All cultures can thrive within a democratic environment and democracy within different cultural settings. The success with which Saudi Arabia has increased participation in its economy and politics shows the extent to which the dominant culture in that country can coexist with democratic arrangements.

As this book becomes available to a larger audience it will add to mutual understanding in the world and thus promote the development of global friendship and solidarity. Prince Faisal deserves our congratulations and thanks for this excellent work of scholarship on political development in Saudi Arabia, a country with an important position in its region and in the world.

—Nelson Mandela

President Nelason Mandela sated a very interesting testimony abdout Saudi Arabia and Gulf sates were he said:

"West must not bluff itself and think that when they talk of democratic government they are superior to the Arab countries. There are certain respects in which the Arab countries, especially the Saudi Arabian kingdom, the United Arab Emirates, Brunei, have served their people in a way which you do not see in the West at all. Saudi Arabia, for example, has free education from the primary level right up to university and at university, the students are given an allowance of $400 a month. They have free health services. There are no taxes. Houses are so heavily subsidized that to get a house is next to nothing. You don't find that in the West. You live at the center of New York and you go to Harlem. You will find that poverty will stare you in the face. Of course we find poverty everywhere, including the Arab countries. But from the point of view of treating their people, the Arabs are doing far better than the West. And talking about Saudi Arabia and UAE, the leader of government has more contact with his people than is done in the West. In Saudi Arabia, the crown prince who is now the virtual ruler, every Tuesday, he sees anybody that wants to see him. He sees thousands, listens to their demands and their complaints, and wherever possible tries to address them. Nothing of the sort in the West. And you must also realize that in a country like the United States of America, you cannot be a mayor, a governor, or a president, if you are not wealthy. I was reading the other day to find that a mayoral campaign cost one candidate $300 million. Where would a common man get $300 million to be able to be a mayor, to be a governor, to be a president? So especially the students, all the of thought must understand what is the world in which they live, and they must not be taken up by propaganda which in many cases is actuated by other interests different from serving the nation"[1].

---

[1] Remarks by Nelson Mandela, at College Park, University of Maryland. November 14, 2001

Decision Making and the Role of *Ash-Shura* in Saudi Arabia

Introduction

Who could have guessed that the message of one unlettered man, known then only as Muhammad Ibn Abd - Allah, who called the people of Arabia to the worship of One God more than 1400 years ago through a Divine Revelation known as the Holy Kurān, would ignite a socio-political revolution that would transcend time and serve as both the catalyst and ideological backdrop for perhaps the most aggressive and unique modernizing project in the Middle East ?

The power of Muhammad's (Pbuh) message is not only to be found in its esoteric qualities, but also in its philosophical brilliance and method of application. No Prophet served his followers in the manner of Muhammad, who was the spiritual teacher and guide as well as statesman and commander of the people's armies. The Prophet Muhammad (Pbuh) established the first Islamic government in the history of the world. In so doing, he established the tradition of Islamic government over Muslim lands and promulgated the laws through which Islamic societies must be governed.

Islamic government is no doubt one of the most important issues of our era, since a growing orthodoxy among Muslims throughout the world, a number of which has reached nearly 1.5 billion, has re-invigorated the faith and the desire of Muslims to live according to the laws and precepts of Islam. There are more than 60 predominantly Muslim States and a growing population of Muslims who are indigenous to the Western countries. Though many erroneously believe that Islam is limited to the Middle East, the fact is that predominantly Muslim countries span the globe covering every region of the East and West. Muslims are the owners of the world's richest stores of natural resources, which include, along with oil and other important minerals, an untapped yet relatively well educated pool of workers. The cost of living in most Muslim countries is very reasonable compared to the cost of minimal existence in the industrialized Western nations, and the people are eager to enjoy economic, technological and scientific advances and development. The extent to which the East and West will co-operatively undertake the development of the Muslim world and facilitate the consumerism of the West is closely tied to the issue of Islamic government.

To those who are unfamiliar with these Islamic laws and principles and who are therefore subject to the numerous and irrational detractions against Islam and Islamic government that have abounded during the twentieth century, this resurgence might be misunderstood and perhaps even be found threatening.

This topic is also important because peaceful co-operation between East and West will be the greatest modern challenge and necessity. The two will neither be able to survive independently of each other, nor will one find it easy or prudent to forcefully attempt to dominate the other. For students of international affairs and diplomacy, policy makers and even business men and women, understanding the diverse cultures and religions of the world in this new century will be as important as understanding the languages and the politics of all nations. In the case of Islam, understanding the Religion is synonymous with understanding the politics of the Region to some degree. Unlike the secular political ideologies that shape the politics of the Western world, Islamic political ideology is grounded in the teachings of the Holy Kurān and the method of governance established by Prophet Muhammad (Pbuh), known as Al Sunna, and to some extent the methods of the Caliphs or rulers who followed him.

The Kingdom of Saudi Arabia has emerged over the past century as one of the largest and most powerful states in the Arab Gulf region. Because of this, its modernising experiences may serve as good examples of Islamic modernisation. Although this book focuses primarily on Islamic political development, the relationship between the politics of the Kingdom, its economy and culture is clear. As stated earlier, the unique aspect of the Saudi modernisation project is its deliberate emphasis on the identity of the people as Arabs and Muslims and its rejection of the concept that modernisation means Westernization.

Saudi Arabia recognized the need to develop a stable basis for lasting social and political progress and prosperity. This recognition was accompanied by the demands of a growing professional and educated Saudi citizenry who are rightly convinced that Islam is capable of yielding guidance and methods towards these ends.

Modern Saudi Arabia has its roots in the rise of Islam. By the time Prophet Muhammad (Pbuh) transcended this life in 632 C.E. (Common Era), most of the Arabian Peninsula had become united under Arab rule. This combination of Arabian culture and Islam has shaped the character of the region ever since.

Although the Arabian Peninsula came under the nominal suzerainty of the Ottoman sultans in Istanbul in the sixteenth century, it remained largely under the rule of various Arab tribes and families, who felt that religion was more important than politics. This importance became very apparent in the eighteenth century when a religious reformer, Mohammed Ibn Abd - al Wahhab, began to preach in favor of a return to the original teachings of Islam, void of innovation, superstitions and idol worship, all of which had found their way into Muslim societies. Ibn Abd - al Wahhab formed an alliance with the Al-Su'ud tribe who at that time dominated much of Najd, the central region of Saudi Arabia. Strengthened by their military and political leaderships Abd - al Wahhab mounted a reform movement that quickly grew and expanded far beyond its base in Najd. In response to this expansion, the Ottoman Empire dispatched troops who defeated the Arab forces yet could not permanently control the area, ultimately yielding control to the Al-Su'ud tribe. Al - Su'uds continued to rule the interior until 1890, when the Rashids, a rival Saudi family, seized control of Riyadh. Then, in 1902, Abd - al Aziz Al - Su'ud (known as Ibn Su'ud) entered Riyadh. regained power over the region. He revived the Arab religious reform movement and established himself as the ruler of Najd.

At the beginning of World War I Abd - al Aziz Al - Su'ud controlled central Arabia and Al-Hasa coast, although the Hejaz and Western Arabia remained under Ottoman rule. In 1916, Hussein Ibn Ali, the Hashemite sheriff of Makkah, proclaimed independence and declared war on the Ottoman Empire, designating himself "King of the Hejaz." In the battles that followed, Hussein liberated much of western Arabia, while Abd - al Aziz subdued Al-Hasa and what remained of Najd, up to the borders of Hejaz. A growing rivalry began between Abd - al Aziz and Hussein after World War I. This resulted in a war that began in 1924, when Hussein proclaimed himself the *Caliph* of Islam. In 1926, Abd - al Aziz attacked Hejaz and conquered Makkah and Jeddah and steadily expanded his rule to include much of western, southern and eastern Arabia. Finally, in 1932, Abd - al Aziz Al - Su'ud announced the unification of all regions into what is now known as the Kingdom of Saudi Arabia.

Of the six Gulf States, Saudi Arabia, Bahrain, the United Arab Emirates, Qatar, Oman and Kuwait, Saudi Arabia is the most heavily populated. Nearly 60% of the total Gulf population now lives in Saudi Arabia.

There is no formal constitution in Saudi Arabia. The laws of Islam provide legitimate guidance for the government and are interpreted by the U'lama, or religious leaders and scholars who form Majlis Ash Shura, as well as scholars from other fields. These constitute the primary mechanism of Saudi political development. Like the other Gulf countries, Saudi Arabia has a long tradition of public access to high officials. This usually occurs through a Majlis (public audience), where citizens have the right to petition officials directly. In 1953, a Council of Ministers was appointed by the King and advised lawmakers and politicians on the formation of general policy. The Council has helped direct the activities of the growing bureaucracy since that time.

Saudi Arabia's brand of monarchy, guided by Islamic laws and precepts, makes it a remarkable example of Islamic politics and development. Its growth and development represent the resurgence or reawakening of Islam, the second largest and fastest growing religion in the world. Scholars from various disciplines are initiating studies on contemporary Islamic phenomena, seeking to understand the implications of Islamic politics from Western perspectives. The home of the annual pilgrimage to Makkah, Saudi Arabia serves as a meeting place for the Muslims of the world. Its potential for leadership in world affairs in the coming century makes it a worthy subject for both academic and practical study.

The Saudi government, like most governments, has been subjected to criticism. The legitimacy of the monarchy has been challenged. The government has been accused of totalitarianism, human rights abuses and the restriction of freedom of speech. It has also been criticized for its co-operative relationships with Western governments during times of political upheaval in the Muslim world. Most of these criticisms are based on lack of knowledge of Islamic Law.

Within the pages of this book, we will define the political A'kida (Creed) and construction of the Saudi political system, based on Shari'a, In doing so, we hope that we will initiate a discussion on Islamic political idealism that will extend beyond these pages and ultimately serve to enlighten both Muslim and non-Muslim students, the Islamic and the Saudi Arabian government, as well as others that take interest in the region.

Chapter ~ 1 ~

Political Development

1-1 Concept

In order to understand the political development of Saudi Arabia, it is necessary to examine alternative concepts of this socio-political phenomenon. Before beginning an analysis of the various concepts of political development, it is important that we determine the meaning of "political development" as used by scholars of political science. The connection between modern organization, specialization, division of labour and professionalism will be addressed within this discussion, as will various political ideologies, specifically Western liberal democracy, Marxism, and Islam. Within the context of various political and economic ideologies and theories, the concept of political development takes on many definitions. Its various dimensions are sometimes common and at other times contrasting. This is an indication that the word "development" is relative and can be interpreted to suit the objectives and desires of specific and general ideals, political and otherwise. As we seek to examine the varying perspectives of writers and scholars on the issue, bureaucracy and political transformation is also examined.

1-2 Definition

The two primary geo-political blocs (East and West), represented by the now defunct Soviet Union and the Western liberal democracies, have historically been divided in accordance with the understanding and objectives of development in both the narrow and broad sense of the term. In respect to economic development, there is a dichotomy between communism, socialism and capitalism. All three have their own unique set of social and political requirements. One common aspect of political development in respect to these three polar concepts, is a preoccupation with the advancement of public policy and the development and establishment of political structures and government organizations that lead to the functional administration of government along specific ideological guidelines.

5

Weber (1971) observed that modern organisations require a high degree of specialisation. He argues that the attributes of modern organisation are public administration of hierarchy, responsibility, rationality, achievement, orientation, specialisation, differentiation, discipline and professionalism. Weber contended that unless public bureaucracies manifest these attributes, they couldn't be effective instruments in bringing about significant economic and socio-political transformation. Weber, having examined the role of bureaucracy in the determination of public policy, stated, "It is obvious, technically, that the great modern state is absolutely dependent upon a bureaucratic basis." At the turn of the century, Weber observed that bureaucracy strives to maximise efficiency and objectivity through impersonality and hierarchical authority relations. Weber claims that the function and structure of a bureaucracy in pursuit of economic development is conditioned by the distribution of power within society and the organisation of the state. He did not ignore the view that bureaucratic organisation is often used as an apparatus for the domination of society. He clearly recognised the significance of bureaucratic tendencies towards domination. Weber asserts that bureaucracy is a form of power, being human, technical and capital resources are organised under a single operating apparatus.

Mills and Gerth (1946) state that Weber speaks of three ideal types of legitimate authority: 1) traditional authority, 2) charismatic authority, and 3) rational-legal authority. Weber's three models present the characteristics of an idealised bureaucracy that represents legitimate authority, yet in reality, none of them exist in a pure form. Mills and Gerth argued that theorists and researchers concerned with the political and economic power of a bureaucracy, have benefited greatly from Weber's ideas. They have served in furthering the understanding of social stratification and power relations in society.

Huntington (1979) defined levels of political institutionalisation in terms of political development, whereas political development according to Bill (1979) is "the capacity of a political system to initiate, absorb, and sustain continuous transformation." Bill submits that it is a process of admitting all groups and interests, including newly recognised interests, into full participation without disrupting the efficiency of the political system and without limiting the ability of the system to choose and pursue policy goals. A higher level of institutionalisation in a political system tends to increase the efficiency of a political - bureaucratic system and its control over the environment, but may fail to meet the test suggested by Bill. Although an institutionalised system is in a better position to rationalise

6

and maximise the use of its country's resources, and in effect create conditions for a more efficient society, Bill's definition of political development remains consistent with the efficiency and capacity of a political system to choose and pursue its public policy goals without disrupting the system itself. If we apply Huntington's institutionalisation criteria of adaptability, complexity, autonomy and coherence to the case of Saudi Arabia, one will find the level of institutionalisation comparatively low. The State, however, has maintained stability while incorporating newly identified interests and groups into society, and continuing an ongoing process of political, social and economic transformation, thereby meeting Bill's definition of political development.

In their review of the literature on political development from the early 1960s until 1975, Huntington and Dominguez (1979) argued that the concept is used in four general ways: 1) geographically, 2) derivatively, 3) teleologically, 4) functionally. Geographical refers to the politics of developing countries in Asia, Africa, the Middle East, and Latin America. In this sense, political development has no specific content or characteristic except that it is connected with poorer and less industrialised countries. The term derivative refers to the linkage of political development to the broader process of modernisation, and often identifies political development with political modernisation. In these cases, the concern is with the transition from a traditional agrarian society to a modern industrial one. Among the other concepts used to make fairly similar distinctions are Migdal's models (1983): elite-mass, diffracted-fused, great tradition-little tradition, urban-rural, and ortho-traditional neo-traditional theories. Riggs (1946), in his discussion on the topic, adds intermediate terms such as transitional or prismatic, which will prove to be theoretically important for studying a society in transition, like Saudi Arabia.

According to Ferre (1984) political development viewed from a teleological perspective is a movement toward one or more goals or states of being within the political arena. The goals may be single or multiple, such as democracy, stability, legitimacy, participation, mobilisation, equality, differentiation, institutionalisation, integration, rationalisation, bureaucratisation and liberty.

The functional aspects of these terms refer to movement toward a certain kind of political system or toward the political characteristics of a modern industrial society. In both Western and Eastern governments, whether democratic or communist, political parties may be considered a functional necessity in a society.

7

If we were to follow these various definitions and approaches closely, we would likely observe that the operational definition of political development used in this study specifically describes political development in the Kingdom of Saudi Arabia. The Kingdom of Saudi Arabia has embarked upon a process or movement away from the status quo and toward new goals and functions for the state. Those new goals and functions referred to here are: nation building, greater participation, integration, and civil liberty.

When defining development in this way, the following two points should be carefully considered: 1. Political development as a first step in transition from the status quo to a new status. 2. Political development is itself a goal; The functions and outcomes of which do not necessarily take place simultaneously.
Some scholars unfortunately use the concept of political development synonymously with nation building, suggesting that the term implies a process of evolution from a previous state of being into a nation state. Hans Kohn (1966) argued that nationalism has been observed as a state of mind in which an individual's supreme loyalty is owed to the nation. Politically, nationalism relates to the awakening and activation of a population during and after a period of colonial domination.

Almond and Powell (1966) defined political development as the consequence of challenges which may emanate from the international environment, the domestic society or the political elite within the political system. In their view, whatever the source, these impulses "involve some significant change in the magnitude and content of the flow of input into the political system." Four types of challenges which exert pressure on any existing political system were identified by Almond and Powell. First, state building, referring to the requirement of increased integration and penetration of the system. Second, nation building, referring to the requirement of greater loyalty and commitment to the system. Third, participation, referring to pressure from groups to have a part in the decision-making process. Fourth, pressure to ameliorate unequal distribution of wealth and income among the people by the state.

Following this same route of analysis, Almond and Powell reach the conclusion: "A political development is a cumulative process of role differentiation, structural autonomy and secularisation. And all are related to system capabilities and system maintenance."

Scholars such as Diamant (1966) saw and defined political development as a process by which a political system acquires the capacity to continuously sustain new types of goals and demands while creating new types of organisation. Eisenstandt (1973) provided a similar definition when he discussed a political system's ability to meet changing demands and then to absorb them in terms of policy making. In this respect, Eisenstandt argued that a political system could assure its own continuity in the face of continuous new demands and new forms of political organisation. Eisenstandt and Diamond equate political development with the ability of political systems to grow or adjust to new demands put upon them. Having found most other meanings partially insufficient, Pye (1966) defined ten major meanings of political development. For Pye, political developments was: "political modernisation, operation of a national state, administrative and legal development, a political prerequisite for economic development, politics typical of industrial societies, mass mobilisation and participation, the building of democracy, stability and orderly change, mobilisation and power and one aspect of a multi-dimensional process of social change."

Other scholars, when focusing on defining political development, centre their attention on other aspects, such as political participation, institutionalisation and integration. Theorists such as Jaguaribe (1973) defined the political development process as political modernisation and political institutionalisation. This theory indicates that political modernisation is a process of increasing the operational variables of a polity. The variables at work are rational orientation, structural differentiation and capability. In addition, this view defined political institutionalisation as the process of increasing political mobilisation, political integration and political representation. Jaguaribe saw political modernisation and political institutionalisation as closely interrelated with political development and requiring an appropriate balance between the two. The greater the imbalance between high levels of modernisation and low levels of institutionalisation, the more dependent the political system will be on the use of violence.

Other writers, such as Binder (1971), viewed political development as "a process of admitting all groups, including newly recognised interests as well as new generations, into full political participation without disrupting the workings of the political system". Without explaining the details of Binder's views, suffice it to say that his views coincide with those of the five other contributors. They reduce political development to the three key concepts of differentiation, equality, and capacity. Collectively, these constitute what is called the "development syndrome". According to Binder (1971) this differentiation refers to a process in

9

society of progressive separation and specialisation of roles, both institutional and associational. The concept of equality as connected with political development has three components: national citizenship, universal legal order and achievement norms. The third key concept "capacity" refers to the ability of a system to innovate, to manage continuous change, to adapt, and to create. He (1967) made an important contribution to the literature of political development. He utilised the concept of differentiation and specialisation, yet did so with a specific concentration on "key governmental technologies", relating these to two additional aspects of political development, equality and capacity. It is evident that Riggs considered these four variables as the collective aspects of political development. He defines key government technologies as bureaucracies, political parties and legislatures. In addition to these, Riggs added a host of minor technologies, one being a test for recruitment. Riggs suggested that judicial procedures exist for the settling of disputes and the creation of private associations and corporations, such as labour unions. For Benjamin, political development is seen as a process of political participation, political institutionalisation and national integration. Needler (1968) shared Benjamin's view, but extended the policy to include the maximum number of participants in the political process in terms of equality.

Thus the endless dispute over the concept of political development continues along the fields and lines of politics and political science. From this brief review of a variety of attempts to define the concept of political development, it is evident that no agreement exists among political scientists as to its exact definition. The concept is loosely used to refer to a process of organic change in the nature of political institutions. There is implicit in any notion, the assumption of cumulative change and growth. Generally speaking, the scholars cited share what might be called a "positive orientation" in the sense that they agree that politics achieve political development, while pointing toward requirements to be met by political systems striving to become politically developed. The stress is on the potentialities for movement from what they consider a less desirable to a more desirable situation in the political system, for example, transition from a non-party to a party system.

Since political development is thought to involve the inclusion into mainstream politics of new groups and interests, some amount of discussion should focus on the impact on society which is felt when groups are prevented from participation or inclusion in the mainstream political culture. Structural differentiation may occur, as well as structural homogenisation. Huntington (1965) argued that national disintegration was as much a phenomenon as national integration; therefore, concepts of political development should be seen as reversible. They should define

10

both political development and circumstances under which political decay is observed. It is evident, therefore, that political development as a concept undergoes a serious stage of complexity of definition to the extent that universal definition may not be attainable. The assumption that a universal or all-embracing definition is preferable does not necessarily mean that such a definition would be helpful or beneficial. This point, however, is open to discussion, since truly universal definitions are impossible to construct due to cultural variations. One can, nevertheless, resort to other forms of definition in order to facilitate the task. This would require the use of stipulated definitions where a relational definition is attempted, giving a description of the attributes of the problem in question. In the case of development, an example might be to consider economic growth and public participation as components of "development."

1-3 Western Point of View

Modern western political development theory dates back to the end of World War Two. Blomstrom and Hettne (1965) noted that the earliest modern theory of development was purely economic and based upon simple modes of growth where capital formation was a key factor. These models were almost entirely based on the economic conditions existing in industrialised Western societies. The authors note that their application of such theories to the problems of the underdeveloped countries revealed an immense gap between fact and theory. Problems with application were compounded by the fact that most third world countries mechanically imitated western methods of study, yet their cultures never yielded to the requirements for successful application.

Most contributions to development theory, whether economic, political, or sociological, originated in a basic paradigm referred to as "the modernisation paradigm. "Development was seen in an evolutionary uni-linear perspective and underdevelopment was defined in terms of observable differences between rich and poor countries. Development in this instance meant the bridging of these gaps through an imitative process through which the less developed countries were expected to become more and more like the industrialised nations. The benefits of modernisation would be, for the most part, taken for granted should emulation occur.

11

Rostow (1965) saw development as consisting of a number of stages which were basically derived from the distinction between "tradition" and "modernity." His approach was probably the most well-known contribution to economic theory within the tradition of modernisation theory. Rostow's doctrine was influential during the late 1950s and early 1960s. It was a typical expression of the western development paradigm. Other western authors focused upon a variety of criteria but most considered political development to be an aspect of modernisation. This characterisation also applies to those scholars within the specialised fields of political development. Most of the major works representing the predominant scholarly perspectives of approaches to the study of political development were written in the 1960s and 1970s. These approaches can be classified as: 1) the historical approach, 2) the structural-functional approach, 3) the normative approach, 4) the institutional and universal approach, and 5) the contextual approach.

1-4 Marxist Point of View

The Marxist approach to the concept of political development reflects another important school of thought Marxism advocates fundamental "structural change" in the political system as a prerequisite for modernisation. Two important categories are observed in this theory. One is the Marxist theory of development, as expounded by Lenin and his followers. The second category is the "dependency movement", with Raoul Prebish (1965) as its first advocate.

In Marxist sociological literature, class is defined in three different categories: wealth, power, and status. Marx contends that there are different bases of power in society. Wealth is but one of the significant variables that determines an individual's position in the class structure. Despite the significance of wealth, it cannot necessarily be translated automatically into power, although it remains a sign of status in society. According to Weber (1971), in modern society, class analysis has been utilised by prominent scholars other than Karl Marx, including David Ricardo and Joseph Schumpter. According to these theorists, economic surplus is utilised for either consumption or production and it shapes the process of economic development. Marx associated class primarily with economic power, which is considered the fundamental base of social stratification. Al Sultan (1988) argues that Max Weber agreed with Marx in that property and lack of property are the basic tools utilised to measure all class structures. Bill (1981) also suggests the incorporation of wealth, power and status into the definition of class. All three dimensions are interrelated in the sense that the possession of one may strongly affect the possession of the other. However, the point is made that wealth is considered one of the most significant variables that determine one's position in the class structure. Thus, the basis of power may be identified as the same for economic, political, social, religious and educational systems. Bill's conceptualisation of class in terms of power is formulated and presented in an attempt to "account for the complexities and subtitles that occur in many stratification systems." An emphasis on power helps incorporate the social and political dimensions of stratification into the analysis along side economic considerations. These factors provide the analyst greater flexibility, making analysis more relevant to the study of different societies.

Bill and Hardgrave (1981) argued that the introduction of a broader definition of class helps to incorporate groups in the study of class structures in a society. They defined class as aggregates of individuals "united by similar modes of employment and maintaining similar power positions in society." This definition of class, according to Bill (1972), does not preclude the study of group since "intra and inter-class analysis is regarded as group analysis." He argues that "group" is defined accordingly as "an aggregate of individuals categorised other than by class who interact in varying degrees in pursuance of common interests." Class is defined in a way that makes room for kinship, tribalism, religious grouping and regional aggregates. Bill and Hardgrave claim that an individual may belong to many groups, but holds membership in only one "class".

When considering national development, the pragmatic revolutionary leader, Lenin, was forced to amend Marx's thesis. Tucker (1979) explained that the capitalist world found ways to lessen the misery of its workers by exporting exploitation to colonies in the Third World. Therefore, Lenin suggests that imperialism is the weakest link of capitalism. He theorized that revolution will erupt in colonies where poverty and underdevelopment are used as tools to further communism. Connor (1968) claimed that the theory of imperialism advanced by Lenin was the "most important single step he took in changing Marxism into an ideology that was relevant to the non-industrialised areas of the world."

13

Lenin's strategy for development became the foundation of the dependency theory and world system approach which can be considered as the main reaction to orthodox views of political development. It is also an attempt to determine the causes and consequences of underdevelopment.

Definitions of "dependency" differ profoundly. For the purposes of discussion, and due to the limitations of time and space, it shall suffice to note that this section does not attempt to identify a common core in the literature or to search for common assertions in dependency linkages.

Some scholars believe that the main argument of dependency theorists was developed by capitalist nations (i.e. the United States and Western Europe) that penetrated the economies of the underdeveloped nations in Africa, Asia, and Latin America, transforming parts of the local economy into modern enclaves, such as the fishing or textile industries. On the other hand, another group of scholars think that many intellectuals from the Developing World in Latin America, Africa and Asia conceptualised the thought of Dependency and World System Approach. This demonstrates the importance of a definition for development from a dependency understanding.

1-5 Islam Point of View

Since the resurgence of Islam in the early 1970s, a wealth of knowledge has emerged. Scholars have shown tremendous interest in the affairs of the Islamic World. In particular, attention has been paid to what is called "Political Islam" in order to investigate the dynamics of Muslim Societies and to understand Islam as a religion, an ideology and a basis for state structure.
As contemporary political scientists progress in their understanding of Islamic political and economic ideology, it has become increasingly apparent that Islam has much to say in respect to development at the economic, social and political levels. Islam is primarily concerned with the salvation of human souls and other esoteric pursuits. Moreover, Islam holds a view of mankind as a total being possessing spiritual and material needs. It produces Islamic principles and methodologies that guide adherents individually and their societies collectively toward both material and spiritual prosperity. (Ahmad, 1997; Fadlallah, 1990; Abd – al majid, 1991).

14

Chapter Tow:
Islamic Political System

2-1: Foundation

Islam shares many common aspects with its ideological counterparts, yet it has its own unique vision with regard to political and economic methodology. The Islamic economic system is concerned with economic independence and self-sufficiency of the populace of the Islamic state, along with the preservation of their inalienable right both to own property and to privately own and control the means of production (Qutb, 1988). Qutb argued that the Islamic government sets limits that discourage corruption, usury and other violations of Islamic law, which inflict undue hardships on the poor, or that limit the rights of people to pursue financial security and advantage according to their output of labour and investment. Islamic law also provides checks and balances for economic systems that are purposefully designed to protect women, children and orphans and their assets (Rahman, 1998).

The foundation of the Islamic political system is *Shura*, which means consultation. This requirement, found in the Kurān and Sunna, distinguishes Islamic political idealism from other ideologies. Whereas Western liberal democracy embodies participative government, the people being the sovereign authority, ruling so to speak by majority vote, Islam requires that government be led by a central authority that recognises God as the sovereign. The human government has an obligation to certain laws and precepts that have been revealed by God (Al-Gazzali, 1971). The Shura or consultative branch of the Islamic government structure, provides a mechanism through which the Islamic government is accessed by the people, not as sovereigns, but as participants, through consultation in government affairs. Thus Islam is against dictatorship and authoritarianism, focusing instead on justice and working for the benefit of the entire society (*Encyclopaedia of Seerah*, 1988).

Issues of succession and legitimacy are key to the stability of the Islamic government and its ability to sustain itself in competition with the secular ideologies. Whereas legitimacy according to democratic ideals is determined by the will of the people, legitimacy of authority in Islam is dependent upon virtue as well (Daiber, 1993). This means that there are only certain people deemed qualified to lead an Islamic state and these qualifications must be met if the government is to be viewed as a legitimate government. What is primary among these virtues is the requirement that all government officials accept that there is only one God, that Mohammed is a prophet of God, and the laws of the Kurān and the teachings of hadith (the sayings of Prophet Mohammed) are the Constitution of any Islamic government (Sahih Muslim). This neither means that a literal interpretation of the Kurān is the basis of Islamic law, nor that implementation in contemporary settings must mimic ancient methods or seek to obtain ancient objectives. Through the use of ijtihad, a tool that is accessible to jurisprudents who interpret and deliberate Islamic law, Islamic law and principles are refreshed from generation to generation (Al-Awani, 1994).

Both the legislative branch of Islamic government and the judiciary branch function in a way that allows government to understand and implement the teachings of Kurān and Sunna in a modern language. The faqih, or jurisprudent in Islam, is charged with the contemporary interpretation of the legal precepts of Kurān. As part of Majlis Ash-Shura, faqihs lend their knowledge and expertise on these subjects to the executive branch and assist in the development of public policies that run parallel with Islamic guidelines. Thus the faqih indirectly facilitates the pursuit of modern goals. (Al-Awani, 1994).

2-2 Islam and Democracy

The Islamic political system is an independent system characterised by freedom from the limitations implied by terminologies found in dictionaries and encyclopaedias of political science. The Western political science concepts of Capitalism, Socialism, Democracy and Totalitarianism have nothing to do with the Islamic political system. There is no room in Islam for these concepts and the Islamic political system can never be associated with the secular political systems implemented in the different parts of the world. (Malik, 1999). No single definition suits every possibility, since Islam allows each Islamic government to shape its character according to the culture of a given people, requiring only the avoidance of prohibited acts, and laws that condone or seek to legalise what the Kurān and Al Sunna have prohibited.

If we accept that one of the fundamental understandings of political development is the ability to make organised changes and achieve political stability while increasing a system's capabilities, we can also accept that Islam is capable of facilitating political growth in a society, and this growth is one of its primary objectives.

Islamic political theory is dependent upon belief and faith in the oneness of God. It approaches from a posture of humility, recognising that the human mind is not capable of understanding or discovering all the possibilities and potentials of life found in the created laws and truths that govern our universe. Only God knows such perfect and complete knowledge. Absolute belief in the oneness of God, unity and the unity of His creation leads to our understanding of the indivisibility of truth and integration of revelation and hypothesis. For this reason, contemporary Islamic political idealism has come to represent the final message in terms of revelation, the Kurān and Sunna - the two divinely revealed sources. These sources cannot be bound by time and place. They represent a conclusive and authoritative communication between God and His prophets, the last of whom was Muhammad. It is essential to this approach that researchers handling theories of political development from the Islamic perspective must look to the Kurān and Sunna as their standard measurement that determines ends, objectives and all truths concerning human beings.

The Islamic perspective observes human phenomena as complex and multi-dimensional. The Islamic political concepts include social, economic and cultural aspects, since politics is defined herewith as administrating issues towards reform, or rather, reforming human beings by directing them to the proper way of life through which they obtain success, prosperity and happiness. The Western concept of politics, however, is limited to discussions of power, authority, class and state.

The Islamic perspective assumes that historical events neither end by vanishing, nor lose relevance in the face of modernity. History in Islam remains alive and relevant in life and memory. Thus, history serves us by allowing us to look back and garner wisdom and direction on the best way to do things and aids us in our understanding of the relationship between cause, effect and consequence.

This connection should always be sought in dealing with current events. For this reason, Muslims view the historic establishment of the first Islamic state as a continuous process guided by a methodology, or Sunna, that will result in the establishment of other Islamic states. This is considered a possibility that is available to Muslims throughout time. Islamation, as some call it, or reclamation, as it is referred to by others, is a process through which Muslims seeks to bring all of creation within the timeless intellectual view of God's revelation.

Islam considers the location of specific political phenomena as a sub-variable, or something that is subject to other dimensions of the human experience. The Islamic view is that political development starts from a position determined by a people's level of awareness and moves from this point of orientation to a clear purpose and transformation, which results in an Islamic nation. As people become more aware of their created nature and the God that created them, they begin to recognise, learn, trust and act upon His guidance. The result is that the people are transformed into an Islamic nation, which is referred to in Islamic terminology as a community of believers, or Ummah.

Depending on the previous definitions elaborated as political development, one can put forward the argument that Islam is both a religion, which touches every aspect of the human being, and a way of life. Muslim states, their governments and rulers are assigned and encouraged to practice, apply and rule according to Islamic regulations on a universal level. According to the Holy Kurān, Islam is a religion and a condition through which Muslims practice social and political affairs in their purest and most perfect way. Thus mankind's efforts to develop the economic, social and political aspects of life are seen as working for the benefit, comfort and welfare of the entire community, Muslims and non-Muslims.

If we take this approach, the notion that Islam is rigid or dogmatic can be refuted.

There is a general agreement among many authors and political science thinkers and theorists that Islam is comprehensive. For these authors and thinkers there is no doubt that Islam compressed faith, ethics, and law as set forth in the Kurān, exemplified by the life of the Prophet Muhammad (Pbuh) and his companions, and later developed by Muslim scholars and jurists (the `ulama' and fuqaha') into the Shari'a *(Law)*, through which Islam provides a unique form of continuous modernisation and progressive attitudes that match modern currents of development and progress. This vocal denunciation of secularism, however, does not imply that these authors make no distinction between the spheres of religion proper and of worldly affairs, between the eternal and the temporal. In fact, this very distinction is reflected in modern Islamic legal theory, which distinguishes between the rituals of worship, which involve a person's interaction with his or her Creator. These rituals are identified essentially as the five pillars of Islam: 1) profession of faith, 2) prayer, 3) fasting, 4) alms giving, and 5) the pilgrimage. This

18

suggests that there are two differentiated spheres of human life and activity: one revolving around faith and worship and the other around worldly affairs. These two spheres are subject to the precepts of Islam. By contrast, secularists believe that the two spheres are separate and that one takes priority over the other. Worldly affairs are subject only to the judgments of human beings who measure all things according to man-made criteria of what is right and wrong. Islam says that mankind must make judgments based on God's criteria of right and wrong.

The hallmark of the truly Islamic system is the application of the Shari'a and not necessarily any particular political order or organisational structure. However, in all instances the elected ruler must be just and he must be subject to *Shura*, taking counsel from the knowledgeable and wise in both spiritual and material sciences. Primary among Islamic state objectives is to fulfil the purpose of the state, utilising the principles upon which it rests. These principles are to be found in the Kurān and Al Sunna, and include most notably: justice, equality, freedom, and struggle in the path of God (*Jihad*). Some go even further in their opinion regarding the objectives of an Islamic state, declaring that any Muslim ruler who does not apply God's criteria of judgment and follow divine law should be considered a sinner, a tyrant, and an infidel; and his rule is illegitimate.

Usually no sharp distinction is made between Islam and the Shari'a, or Islamic law. As a rule, both terms are used interchangeably. In accordance with the functional theory of government, Shari'a is the cornerstone of an Islamic order. The government is merely the executor of God's law. The current debate among Islamic political scholars focuses whether the Shari'a should be defined as a comprehensive set of norms and values regulating human life to the most minute detail, or as a set of strict and pre-established laws. There is a general consensus that the Shari'a is comprehensive but at the same time flexible, and therefore suited for all times, places and circumstances. This leads to the crucial distinction between an untouchable and immutable core that has been decisively defined by God's word and the Shari'a's flexible components. Its modern interpretation is derived by human reason from an ancient presentation, thus rendering a contemporary Islamic jurisprudence through the utilisation of *Ijtihad*.

This distinction provides one of the criteria by which one may delineate conservatives, modernists, and progressives. The aim of "enlightened" modernist reformers has, of necessity, been to define the scope of human interpretation as extensively as possible. This endeavour was characterised somewhat uncharitably

19

by Keir as an attempt to define the Shari'a primarily as being full of "empty spaces." Such criticism is looked upon as a lack of knowledge about Islam.

In the case of politics, the Ulama, or scholars who qualify as conservatives on the basis of their social views, hold remarkably modern ideas that applying the Shari'a requires social organisation and a state. But God in his wisdom left the details of political organisation of the Muslim to the Muslims' discretion, allowing Muslims to interpret, advance, or suspend certain law according to the societies' needs and aspirations. Government and politics are part of the Mu'amalat (administrative procedures) that are to be regulated so as to realise the common good which, if properly understood, coincides with the purposes, (maqasid), of the *Shari'a.*

Whilst the Islamic state is central to the enforcement of Islamic law, its form and organisation are declared decentralized as a matter of technique. This has to be seen in relation to the common assertion that Muslims are not prohibited from adapting techniques and modes of organisation of non-Islamic origin, provided they do not contradict Islamic values. If government organisation is a matter of convenience and mere technique, then the adoption of democracy, or of certain democratic elements, may be acceptable, recommended, or even mandatory provided this does not lead to the neglect or violation of Islamic norms and values. Western secular liberalism, with its base rooted in the ideal that man is sovereign, is of course incompatible with Islamic values or political idealism. Yet this is not the only form of democracy, assuming that the term democracy is merely representative of participative and representative government. The simple conclusion is that Islam, as a state and as a religion, works and provides for economic, social, and political development at all times, levels and locations. It is neither authoritarian, nor is it democratic in the Western sense. An Islamic state avoids the disadvantages of either system.

2-3 Sovereignty and Legitimacy in the Muslim State

Muslim governments may differ in their structures from those of other states. The general framework of all authorities in a Muslim state makes that the state emerge from a set of divine laws, upon which are based the purposes, politics and even behaviour of Muslims. Accordingly, all Muslims should adhere to the divine laws. From an Islamic perspective it can also be argued that basic factors such as people, land and political authority are not enough to establish a Muslim state. In addition to such materialistic factors, an establishment of an Islamic state requires statistical factors, called "the legal status of the Muslim state". There has to be a set of principles and rules stipulated by Islam based on the purpose, as well as a definition of the relationship between the governed population and those who govern. Since divine laws govern a Muslim state, Muslim communities are not authorised to change these laws; even the authorities in the Muslim state are not allowed to alter them. The sovereignty of a Muslim state is directly related to the law and revelation of God (Anaadi, 1999). An Islamic state and its position regarding a present political system should not be characterised or defined by any of the terminologies approved by any mandated political theory (e.g. democracy, socialism etc). It is also unacceptable to attribute political legitimacy to a system simply because it calls itself an Islamic state. Unless it is recognised that the Islamic state is distinctive and differs from all present non-Islamic states, as a matter of both conduct and ideology, a number of issues will continue to be viewed as contradictory. An Islamic-state, for example, is a state that combines religious doctrine and public policies, while respecting the opinion of the majority in a form similar to present day Western democratic systems.

Sovereignty, as Jean Bodin proclaims it, is a relatively modern theory; but Jean-Jacques Rousseau was the one who has spread this approach within democratic thought. According to Annadi (1999) two theories developed from Rousseau's approach: 1) the sovereignty of the nation, and 2) the sovereignty of the people. This approach was not known to early Muslim philosophers simply because that concept was not a controversial issue in their societies. Besides, the first Islamic state, as Prophet Muhammad (Pbuh) established it, did not have any problem related to the issue of sovereignty. The issue of sovereignty wasn't raised until recent times, under the influence of Western political concepts, theories, and experiences. In Western states, the issue of sovereignty was raised because rulers claimed that they ruled "in the name of God." A conflict between rulers and their subjects continued until some political theorists proclaimed the separation of the king from legislative power and the clergy. Among those theorists are Luke in England and Mistseko and Zussea in France. They sought to define the role of the rulers in a way that undermined the principle of the sovereignty of the king (Abu Eid, 1989). This approach paved the way for a number of revolutions in both the 17th and 18th centuries. People in Europe revolted against the tyranny of the kings and their confiscation of the freedom of the public.

Rulers in Muslim states did not proclaim such divine sovereignty (Kung, 1986). They ruled their people within the range of the people's inalienable rights. Even though some rulers transgressed their limits and abused the implementation of the laws of Islam, this never became a norm in Islamic government and the Shari'a has maintained its validity as the rule of law in the Muslim society (Abu Eid, 1989). Muslim rulers never enjoyed the authority of legislation as practised in medieval Europe. Scholars and those who were well versed in Kurān and the traditions of Prophet Muhammad (Pbuh) used to decide on matters that were not mentioned in the two fundamental religious sources of Islam. They practised this approach based on defined methodological regulations that guarantee no violation of the basic divine laws of Islam. Those scholars did not tackle the issue of human sovereignty because it was not of any concern to their society.

Contemporary Muslim scholars question the compatibility of human sovereignty with the laws of Islam. Annadi (1999) discussed several trends in Islamic thinking. The first being the sovereignty of the nation. Some Muslim scholars argue that sovereignty is based on the well being of the nation as long as it keeps itself within the framework of Shari'a. They believe that this perception of sovereignty is justified as long as it is founded on this principle. Once it transgresses the limits of Shari'a and does not accord with the welfare of the nation, it loses its legitimacy. This approach argues that the Muslim nation is the source of sovereignty in any Muslim state. But this approach is rejected because the only sovereignty accepted by Muslims is the sovereignty of God. No nation can claim that it enjoys sovereignty similar to that of God. A second trend says the source of sovereignty is God. It is the belief in this approach that God stipulates and ordains the behaviour and destiny of both rulers and the general public. Once sovereignty is attributed to any party (e.g. the nation rather than God), a violation of the basic religious principle of Islam occurs. Thirdly, there is the theory of double sovereignty. Advocates of this approach believe that sovereignty in Islam is founded on two points: i) absolute sovereignty represented in the Kurān and the traditions of Prophet Muhammad (Pbuh), and ii) limited public sovereignty represented by the majority of Muslims, provided there is no religious text in the Kurān to annul this right. This double approach can be attributed to the fact that Islam does not leave people to run their affairs according to their own whims, while it recognizes the legitimacy of decisions arrived at through consensus.

Proponents of this approach do not support the idea of public sovereignty, yet they maintain that Islam does not deny a form of rule based on the vote of majority. The justification for this approach is found in the sayings of the Prophet Muhammad (Pbuh). For example "God supports a collective stand by the group" and "The nation of Islam can never collectively approach a misdemeanour". Of course, based on this analytical understanding of the issue of collective opinion in Islam, it can be argued that the principle of consultation in Islam has emerged as a lawful approach, and satisfies the requirement for representation without denying the protection of the polity from ill-advised and trendy experimentation fomented by public opinion.

Close scrutiny of the "double sovereignty" theory would lead us to results that are utterly unacceptable. We might discover through careful examination that the approach is being strongly influenced by subjective beliefs, such as the theory of the sovereignty of the people. Advocates of this approach tried to establish some legal or philosophical base for the issue of sovereignty in Islam, making their approach even more complex. To argue that sovereignty is common between God and those who are governed is unacceptable, for it divides sovereignty equally between God and the people, and in some cases gives the popular majority greater sovereignty than God. This falls in contradiction to the principle of Islam that accepts that God Almighty is the sole sovereign and his sovereignty is individual. Individuals might exercise various roles in a society, but their actions must be regulated by a secure and divine mechanism. Annadi (1999) argued that to reach a precise solution to the problem of sovereignty, there is a need to differentiate between the source of sovereignty and a party that has the right to exercise sovereignty. This meaning a party upon which some amount of sovereignty has been conferred. He asserted that the source of sovereignty could be defined as represented in the divine entity. That is because every act and the human will, derive their actuality and legitimacy from God. This sort of sovereignty is indivisible and absolute. This sovereignty leaves room for human beings to utilise their logic in deciding matters provided whatever they decide does not contradict the basic laws of God. Addressing the question "Who has the right to exercise sovereignty in a Muslim state?" Annadi argued that it is the members of the Islamic nation who can exercise such a right. The right is not exclusive to one particular individual or sect. This situation necessitates a central public authority, and the responsibility to establish such an authority lies with the Islamic nation at large. This Islamic approach to sovereignty is embodied within a tight framework and a defined system of law and tradition stipulated by God. It allows people a limited space in which they are to behave in a manner that never transgresses the limits so defined. It recognizes the imperfection of the human being and seeks to limit the ill affects of imperfection by guiding adherents to depend upon a perfect law upon which to order our lives and the societies in which we live. Since

23

mankind is incapable of perfection, understanding or applying the law perfectly is outside of our capacity. Error is covered by God's promise to forgive and protect the righteous and those who follow them in the pursuit of righteousness through obedience to the law. This cover of protection is denied to those who wilfully reject the Divine law, or their obligation to submission. The divine sovereignty has defined the rights and freedom of the public in a way that guarantees the happiness of people in their life on earth and their life after death. Thus, no gap is left for the practice of tyranny or oppression. Islam does not restrict the freedom of the general public; this freedom is restricted only according to the demands of the public interests of Muslim societies.

2-4 Legitimacy of Authority in Islam

At this point of analysis there is a need to define sources of the laws of Islam (Sharia). They are the Kurān and the sayings and traditions of Prophet Muhammad (Pbuh), which include Qiyas and Ijmaa. The term Qiyas means that Muslim scholars, or individuals, who are well versed in Islam may weigh individual cases by comparing them with established religious principles. These principles should have been approved either by the Prophet Muhammad (Pbuh) or his follow companions. The term Ijmaa refers to a collective opinion concluded and adopted by Muslim scholars after deliberation, consultation and exchange of religious points of views. The Ijmaa, adopted by the majority of Muslim Scholars, is authoritative and should be observed and respected in all its related social practices.

The issue of legitimacy tops the list of quantitative solutions for a given political problem. This is because legitimacy is the supportive pillar of any modern state; it obliges people in office to abide by a legal framework. This adherence also prevents them from claiming the right to rule eternally. Secondly, legitimacy is the basic foundation of any principle of political organisations. Thus, legitimacy is the common denominator which determines the strength of all political organisations.

There was pre-Islamic attention given to legitimacy. Islam mandates that public officials conduct their private and public affairs according to the values and norms of the Kurān and the traditions of Prophet Muhammad (Pbuh). According to Abd - al Hafiz (1996), the implication of the political problem questions the means that,

24

if practised, would block any sort of tyranny in the practice of authority. Rulers in any Muslim society should abide by the rule of the Kurān and the traditions of Prophet Muhammad (Pbuh) and in return their subjects should offer them obedience. The continuity of any authority in office in a Muslim nation is dependent upon the government's adherence to the laws of Islam.

All rules stated in the Kurān and the traditions of Prophet Muhammad (Pbuh) should be applied and practised on an equal basis. Abd - al Hafiz (1996) argued that the ruler represents the principle of legitimacy in Islam in a way that establishes an Islamic society as depicted in both the Kurān and the traditions of Prophet Muhammad (Pbuh). Based on this approach, it can be argued that legitimacy becomes a norm against which the validity of the government is measured by. Its legality is judged accordingly. Together with this standard of legitimacy exists the requirement that an Islamic government come to power through Islamic methods and with the intention to establish itself as an Islamic authority.

Chapter Three:

Saudi Arabia: History and Legitimacy

3-1 History

The Kingdom of Saudi Arabia occupies more than three-quarters of the Arabian Peninsula. It consists of 2,630,000 square kilometres, which is about nine times the area of the British Isles. It borders Kuwait, Iraq and Jordan in the north, Yemen and Oman in the south and the United Arab Emirates and Qatar as well as the Arabian Gulf in the east. The Red Sea borders the Kingdom of Saudi Arabia to the west.

Saudi Arabia is divided into five geographical regions: Asir, which is the southern region; the northern region along the borders of Jordan and Iraq; Najd or the Central region; Hejaz, the western region along the Red Sea; and Al-Hassa, which is the eastern region.

3-1-1 Central Arabia (*Najd*)

Muslim historian Al-Rehani described Najd as "the highland". It consists mainly of sedimentary plateaux interspersed with sand deserts and low isolated mountain ranges. It extends as far as the Rub-Al-Khali Desert in the south, which forms its only natural boundary, while its other boundaries are the Nafud desert to the north, Al-Dahna desert to the east and the Hejaz to the west.

Al Riyadh, the capital city of Saudi Arabia, is the largest city in Najd. In Arabic, Riyadh means 'the garden'. This name is due to the number of vegetable gardens and date groves located in the Wadi Hanifeh.

3-1-2 Western Saudi Arabia (*Al Hijaz*)

The Western region of Saudi Arabia is traditionally described as having two parts. One of these parts is the Hejaz, which means "barrier" in Arabic. The Hejaz extends from the Jordanian borders on the Red Sea in the north, to Taif in the south. It includes the two most holy cities of Islam, Makkah and Medinah.

Makkah is the most important city in the Muslim world as it is the home of the *Kaba*, a religious shrine and place of pilgrimage or Hajj. Every Muslim, if physically and financially able, must perform Hajj, which is the 5th pillar of Islam, at least once in a lifetime.

Makkah is also the place at which the preaching of the Prophet Muhammad (Pbuh) first began and is also the place of his most important victory, since it was the center of commerce and power during Arabia's pre-Islamic period. The acceptance of Islam by the people of Makkah was a significant milestone in the progress of the Islamic faith.

Al-Medinah is the city to which the Prophet Muhammad (Pbuh) migrated, escaping from the Qurayish rulers of that time. Upon his migration to Al-Medinah, which was previously known as Yathrib, the Prophet established the first Islamic community and government. The Prophet's mosque was established in Al-Medinah and the majority of the 23 years of Muhammad's prophethood was experienced there. *Al-Medina* is very important, since it is a place of both Islamic historical significance and religious reverence. Most pilgrims include a visit to this very important city in their Hajj.

The Hejaz was conquered by King Abd - al Aziz in 1925 and has been a part of the Saudi state since that time. Jeddah, on the Red Sea coast, was the center for foreign embassies in Saudi Arabia until the 1970s when the embassies were moved to Riyadh, the capital of the country.

3-1-3 Southern Saudi Arabia *(Asir)*

Asir means "difficult" or "dangerous" in Arabic. It is now the name of the center of the southern region of Saudi Arabia. It was conquered by King Abd-al Aziz in the 1930s. Asir is characterised by its high and steep mountains that face the Red Sea in the west and slope down to Jizan, a modest city on the coast. In the east, the mountains slope down gradually towards Najd and Rub-Al-Khali desert. On top of the Asir mountains sits the city of Abha, the region's largest city.

3-1-4 Eastern Saudi Arabia

Eastern Saudi Arabia covers the area between the Al-Dahna Desert and the Arabian Gulf. Nakhle, which is now called the Eastern Region of Saudi Arabia and is the largest oasis in the world, used to cover the major part of an area on the west coast of the Gulf, extending from Basra in the north to Oman in the south and was originally called *"Al-Bahrain"*.

Al-Hassa means "water under sand and on top of a hard surface". It is an agricultural area, with abundant water springs. Al-Hofuf, Al-Qateef, Al-Oqair and

27

Al-Jubail are some of its major old cities. Dammam, Dahran, Khobar and Ras Tanoura are the new cities in this region and were developed as a result of oil exploration in the area. Al-Hassa was conquered by King Abd al Aziz Al-Su'ud in 1913.

3-1-5 Northern Saudi Arabia

Northern Saudi Arabia extends along the Kingdom's northern frontiers with Iraq and Jordan. Its major cities are Ha'il, Al-Jawf, Skaka, Arar and Qurayat. Tabuk is the largest city of this region. Ha'il is the city of origin of the Al-Rasheed family who controlled Najd during the latter stage of the Second Saudi state. King Abd al Aziz recaptured Riyadh from the Al-Rasheeds in 1902.

Saudi Arabia is the largest country in the world without permanent rivers. The annual rainfall averages approximately 5.9mm. In Asir, the annual rainfall can reach 91mm. The weather is mostly desert-like, and characterised by extreme cold in the winter. Temperatures can reach as high as 49°C on summer days, and may drop below freezing in the winter. On the Red Sea and the Gulf, relative humidity reaches 100% most of the year.

3-2 Population and Economy

The most recent census in Saudi Arabia, which was conducted in 1992, reported a Saudi population of over 12 million people and an expatriate population of 4,624,450. Historically the Saudi economy previously depended mainly on agriculture and herd raising. Revenues from the pilgrimage of Muslims to Makkah were also a major source of income to the Kingdom.

However, since the discovery of oil and its production, which began after the Second World War, the economy changed, as did almost every other aspect of life in the country. The Saudi Arabian Monetary Agency Report 1999 shows that the average oil production in 1998 was 8.28 million barrels per year while the proven reserves reached 259,200 million barrels. Over the last 30 years the Kingdom initiated six development plans aimed at improving the economy by changing the country's economic base and encouraging more manufacturing. (Ministry of Planning, 1996).

28

A full understanding of the social and political changes that have emerged in this country is not possible outside a historical discussion of successive events. The story of Saudi Arabia and its beginnings as a small principality named Dariya is seldom mentioned outside of Arab academic circles. Yet the history of this desert Kingdom is as exciting as it is important, since the history is filled with intrigue, conquest and the character of a proud and sturdy people. Ibrahim Ibn Musa was the securely ensconced ruler of the principality known as Dariya[i]

It was never challenged by outside forces and so Ibrahim steadily expanded his influence beyond his narrow borders. One of his sons, Abd-al-Rahman, founded and established the settlement of Dhurma, which was destined to play an important role in the subsequent history of the area.

Al-Rihani, in his historic recollection, says that another son of Ibrahim Musa named Saif, was the progenitor of the Abuyahya settlers of Abd - al Kabash, which is north of Dariya and a rather mysterious ruin with a great clay mound composed of the disintegrated walls and towers of an older fort. Abd - Allah, a third son, was the ancestor of Al-Watban. The fourth son, Markhan, deserves honourable mention as the progenitor of the Saudi family tree through his younger son Migrin, whose son Muhammed, was the father of the first Su'ud.

3-3 The First and Second States

According to Kostiner, (1990) "Su'ud, Son of Mohammad, who was the son of Migrin, was the founder of a state that in spite of many tribulations, took hold of ancient Dariya, and reached its zenith during the long and glorious reign of Abd - al Aziz Ibn Su'ud. It was in 1721AD during his grandfather's reign in Dariya that the late King's almost equally famous namesake, the first Abd - al Aziz, son of Mohammed Ibn Su'ud was born. Su'ud himself was not destined to see the flowering of his progeny; nor could he have been aware of the existence, in the neighbouring town of Ayaina, of a young and earnest theological student whom destiny had cast in the role of guide, philosopher and friend of both his son and grandson. This was Mohammad Ibn Abd al-Wahhab, who was born at Ayaina in 1703".

Mohammed Ibn Su'ud, the ruler of *Dariya* adopted the call of the preacher Sheikh Mohamed Ibn Abd-al Wahhab in 1745 and offered him support.

Unlike the familiar alliances that took place between tribes or princes in those days, the alliance between Ibn Su'ud and Sheikh Abd al Wahab was an alliance between a religious reformer and a political leader, which was seen as an alliance between the "*Kurān* and the sword". Al-Shalboub, commenting on this situation said: "This alliance paved the way for what has been known as the first Saudi state."

The first Saudi state witnessed harsh and adverse conditions, yet the members of the Saudi state proved to be heroes who strived to unite the tribes of central Arabia and to plant the seed of a strong government that would be inherited by their descendants.

Table 3.1 The Rulers of the First Saudi State

1.	Muhammad Ibn Su'ud	1726 - 1765
2.	Abd al Aziz Ibn Muhammad	1765 -1803
3.	Su'ud Ibn Abd al Aziz Ibn Su'ud	1803 -1814
4.	Abd - Allah Ibn Su'ud Ibn Abd al Aziz Muhammad Ibn Su'ud	1814 - 1818

The reign of Abd al Aziz Ibn Su'ud reached the frontiers of Damascus in the north and the Rub Al-Khali in the desert south and the Red Sea in the west to the Gulf sea shore in the east. The second Imam of this state, Abd al Aziz Ibn Su'ud, was killed in 1803, and his son Su'ud took over. It was during Su'ud's era that the state witnessed its maximum expansion. He personally led most of the military expeditions and was recognised as a religious personality and a skilled fighter. The land of Su'ud extended from Oman and Hadramaut valley to Najran, and from Asir at the shores of the Euphrates to the Syrian desert near Damascus and from the Gulf to the Red Sea.

This episode of dynastic rule was shaken by Egyptian-Turkish occupation and siege which the Turks imposed on Dariya in 1818. The siege brought a tragic end to the rule of Al-Su'ud. Five years later, after re-grouping and reinforcement of religious support, the Saudi rulers were able to restore their rule. The second generation of Al-Su'ud rulers established their Kingdom on the ruins left by the Turks. Turki Ibn Abd - Allah Ibn Mohammad Ibn Su'ud, empowered with the help, love, admiration and respect of the people, established the second Saudi state in 1823.

The sacrifices of Al-Su'ud rulers gave them a recognized right to govern the Kingdom. Their empowerment was also based on their love for the people, adherence to the basic laws of Islam, respect for the Sheiks or the heads of the tribes, the peoples' belief in the noble purpose of the state and the sense of common purpose that combined religious momentum with political and patriotic objectives. The traditional system of role continued up to the inception of the second Saudi state, which lasted from 1823 – 1843.

Table 3.2   Rulers of the Second Saudi State

1.	Turki Ibn Abd Allah Ibn Muhammad Ibn Su'ud	1824 – 1833
2.	Faisal Ibn Turki Ibn Su'ud	1834 – 1838
3.	Khalid Ibn Su'ud Ibn Abd Al Aziz Ibn Muhammad Abd - Allah Ibn Thunyan Ibn Ibrahim Ibn Thunyan Ibn Su'ud	1841 - 1843

Subsequent Saudi rulers benefited from the experiences of their predecessors and used the experience that they gained to bring changes in the system of administration, tax-levying, the regional House of Court and the judges. They reinforced the loyalties extended by the people to their grandfathers and were able to restore the shattered fortunes of the Saudi state, which restored the dignity and prestige of the Al-Su'ud state.

The period from 1838 to 1843 witnessed dramatic moves that were rooted in the return of the Turks led by Mohammed Ali Pasha with the aid and assistance of Khalid Ibn Su'ud who took over when Faisal Ibn Turki left for Egypt. The decades to follow were a period of unrest that included the seizure of Riyadh by

Ibn Rasheed, who took this opportunity to establish the House of Rasheed and nearly eliminate the second Saudi state in 1891.

3-4 The Modern Saudi State: 1902 to the Present Day

After a prolonged period of miserable and difficult years of exile, Prince Abd al Aziz Ibn Su'ud managed to restore the rule of Al-Su'ud in the city of Riyadh in the year 1902. It has been said that Abd al Aziz Ibn Su'ud was a man of destiny. He used spiritual weapons, so to speak, to establish peace and order in the midst of anarchy. It seems he was destined to guide his people out of obscurity and poverty into prosperity, for it was during his reign that the virtue of the desert culture came inevitably into contact with, and under the influence of modern materialism.

A flood of modern innovations very rapidly swept away many of the landmarks of ancient social customs and practices. The economic climate of the Saudi Kingdom had changed beyond recognition and these changes to some extent were permanent, since they resulted from the natural transformation of a society from antiquity to modernity. Abd-al Aziz Ibn Su'ud left a series of challenges to be inherited by his successor. Among these challenges were the early struggles against parochial enemies, the management of the succeeding stage of expansion on an international scale and the consolidation of the tribes. All these activities, occupying the space of about forty years, played an important role in the chronological changes and developments realized by the Saudi state. In 1930 there was nothing to suggest that the new era would be markedly different from anything that had preceded it. Although some rigid aspects of the movement had been abandoned as a matter of policy, there was to be no slackening in the respect owed to Islam by the Saudi people, nor in the strict observance of its precepts and obligations by all who sought the hospitality of Arabia.

The economic situation has changed drastically in the Kingdom. In 1942 Abd - al Aziz Ibn Su'ud was at the peak of his career and reputation; however, some ten years earlier he had taken a characteristically unorthodox decision, which cast its shadow into the future. He had allowed Americans to enter his realm in search of oil. It was found, but the development of its potential was soon halted by the out break of World War Two.

Saudi Arabia relegated to the doldrums of penury as the flow of pilgrims to Makkah had been discontinued during the war. Ibn Su'ud, who had sustained the country comfortably in the old days on a budget of L 100,000 a year and had become accustomed to annual revenue of fifty times that amount, was in despair. The oil began to flow in a satisfying trickle. The King understood the importance of money, though he never abandoned the simplicity of manners to which his upbringing had accustomed him. Ibn Su'ud was famous for his generosity and hospitality.

During the last few years of his life, when the signs of economic decline were too obvious to escape anyone's notice, there was a general relaxation of discipline and control, with disastrous effects on the reputation of the country. Nevertheless, Ibn Su'ud could rise to majestic heights of wrath or eloquence under the provocation of some heinous crime against the Islamic moral code. His presence was always a warning to the would-be transgressor.

When the old King passed away, the tasks awaiting the next regime were formidable. This point of historic development marks an end of a chain of events that paved the way for the emergence of different types of change. No one understood these changes better than the new King Su'ud, Ibn Su'ud's eldest surviving son and successor. He was the fourth of his name to rule in Arabia. Su'ud had shared his father's responsibilities for nearly twenty years before being called upon to assume the major burden himself with the support of his brother, Amir Faisal, who was Crown Prince.

In spite of various ill-founded contentions, there was never any indication of trouble over the succession. The King's huge family was so united in loyalty to him that the possibility of a challenge to the arrangements prescribed by him for the future of the Kingdom could not have been countenanced. The country was in urgent need of a properly constituted government which would be in a position to manage the period of transition following the King's demise. When a government was formed under the authority of the Crown Prince, the King's death occurred before it had time to take shape. The affairs of the state took a back seat while the new King, Su'ud, was busy assessing the situation. His assistants, under the presidency of the new Crown Prince, were directed to overhaul the administrative machine, while he himself made extensive tours of the kingdom, his objective being to see the people and to be seen by them. He made visits to Egypt and Pakistan and met the king of Jordan. This move provided opportunities to take stock of Saudi Arabia's international commitments. There were also consultations with the rulers of Bahrain, Kuwait, Qatar and Yemen. Relations with the new regime in Syria and with Lebanon also came under review.

The King never spared himself in his efforts to measure up to his responsibilities. In his book *Arabia Unified*, Al-Mana says that it was only four months after the King's accession that the new government was formally inaugurated by him with the customary pomp and ceremony which included a speech from the throne indicating the direction in which the King and his advisers were thinking. It was made quite clear at this time that the country would no longer be left to the mercies of the Finance Ministry, which was to be dismembered and its fragments distributed among other departments, including those to be newly created. Two of the King's brothers were nominated as ministers, while the King himself and the Crown Prince remained President and Vice President of the Council of Ministers respectively.

The financial situation in the country at that time could scarcely be regarded as satisfactory, even though the country was rich beyond the wildest dreams of its early founders. The test of a King's capacity to rule must primarily depend on his will and the ability to root out corruption in the government. Fundamental to the discussion introduced so far, is the fact that the future of the new Saudi government, under His Majesty King Su'ud IV, depended entirely on his capacity to grapple with the problems of domestic administration. The traditional anarchy of the Bedouin tribes did more harm to the reputation of the country than the wild men of the desert had done in thousands of years. Yet there were signs of an incipient recognition of this distressing fact at the highest levels of authority. Moreover, it was a good augury that the king had taken one decision which would at least lighten the heavy burden of his crown which stands as a striking early example of political reform. He divested himself of the responsibility for the conduct of the administration by relinquishing the Presidency of the Council of Ministers in favour of the Crown Prince Amir Faisal Ibn Abd -al Aziz Ibn Su'ud.

3-5 The Expansion of the Realm

Religion is central to the process of development in Saudi Arabia. It explains and defines both the moral and political idealism of Saudi rulers. Since consultation (Ash-Shura) is exhorted by the Kurān, Muslims view it as a divine order that should be observed by any Muslim ruler. Throughout the line of Al-Su'ud succession, the implementation of this divinely ordained process has been strictly observed. King Abd al Aziz, like his forefathers, never undertook any enterprise without consulting religious and tribal leaders. With an adherence to the principle of consultation, the early Saudi state, which was the infant of the modern Saudi state, made remarkable progress in its expansion far beyond expectations. Thus, the legitimacy of the Al-Su'ud monarchy emerged from its adherence to the principle of consultation as stated in the Holy *Kurān* and earned the monarch the support of the Saudi people. In Arabia, besides being the Imam of his people, the ruler was and is commonly referred to as "Al Sheikh", while the only other person in the realm entitled to such distinction would be the acknowledged heir to the throne.

It was and still is the aim of Saudi rulers to work relentlessly to sustain past achievements, which include the unification of the tribes and the promulgation of a body of civil law based on the Kurān and Al Sunna of the Prophet. The piety and charity of Abd al Aziz cannot be doubted. His self appointed task of "commanding virtue and condemning vice" always needed the aid of his strong right hand to protect the weak against the strong. Abd al Aziz always faced that task without flinching. His patience with rebels against his authority, even under the gravest provocation, was perhaps as remarkable as his generally successful force in taming the wild men of his land. Taxes were paid regularly and his call on the towns and tribes for the amounts to which the state was entitled in connection with its military activities were generally paid promptly. The State was prosperous enough in a modest way, though its expenditure on religious establishments and education must have absorbed a large percentage of the country's revenue. This approach to government spending bolstered the citizen's conviction regarding the legitimacy of the ruler who utilised all possible efforts to implement the laws of Islam and Al Sunna of the Prophet. The Prophet's first official acts when he migrated to Al-Medinah and established the first Muslim community, was to establish a mosque and then a school.

Modern reforms evolved in response to the conditions of a desert country; which predated the Saudi reform movement. Many of the subsequent reforms were in response to the flood of wealth that marked the period following the Second World War. In our analysis of the changes that came through reform, was the psychological make up of Saudi citizens. One example of this psychological disposition is the fact that the people, who in the past had suffered from many natural calamities like famine, locusts and pestilence, never had any economic reasons for dissatisfaction with their government, which rose and fell mainly as the result of personal, rather then political problems. The people were satisfied that government leaders were devoted to them and ruled the Kingdom with their best interest at heart, even though their ruling was naturally imperfect. In the modern form of governmental administration, some features of the old methods still survive in spite of the modernisation of living conditions. An example of this is the State's obligation to maintain such services as the ecclesiastical administration, charity and hospitality.

Today, Saudi Arabia is ruled in the presence of numerous and critical spectators, and under very different conditions. It should be known that Saudi rulers are aware of their rights and obligations. Ibn Su'ud was an example of a democrat familiar with the processes of consultation. Consultation, as an Islamic principle, means giving the public a chance to participate in governmental affairs. The principle of consultation (Ash-Shura) has been and still is an integral element of Arab Muslim life. Ibn Su'ud himself often referred to a quotation from the Kurān that says: *"Take counsel among yourselves, and if they agree with you, well and good, but if otherwise, then put your trust in God, and do that which you deem best" (Surah Ash-Shura).*

3-6 The Early Administrative Mechanism

The early Saudi rulers, without exception, intended to establish Islam, and they proposed to accept full responsibility for doing so properly. These developments were not merely nominal, but reflected the decision of all early Saudi rulers to bring their territories under a homogeneous administrative system, particularly in the fields of finance and budgeting which were somewhat haphazard and at the mercy of provincial governors. Thus the old order was steadily yielding to the new and the Saudis were considerate and astute enough to make allowances for their old and loyal colleagues during the period of their incumbency. Governors were responsible for collecting the revenues of their provinces and remitting a fixed portion to the central treasury. What remained was a Governor's own salary and allowances, out of which he had to meet all the expenses of his administration. Modeled by early Saudi structures, this system was notoriously inefficient and corrupt. Its major defects have been entirely eradicated in the Arab lands. Nevertheless, in view of the new role which Saudi Arabia would play in the international and economic schemes, it was inevitable that her administrative machinery should be adjusted to the needs of the modern world. Furthermore it was obvious that, in order to have people who were able to operate the new machinery, some modifications in the educational system were essential.

In the past, education was seen as exclusively concerned with the Arabian humanities, with religion at the center. Avenues leading from there into every branch of intellectual speculation suggested by Kurānic and traditional texts developed in the voluminous literature of the exegetes, the historians, the geographers, the philosophers, the scientists, and others, which also included the pre-Islamic poets of the Arabian golden age. Al-Rihani (1970) talks about that change in education from another perspective. He argues that the need for modern education was not felt in Saudi Arabia before the conquest of Hejaz and that an urgent need for secular education was readily admitted as a desirable sequel to traditional subjects. Unfortunately, education had to be sought abroad, owing to the lack of suitable teaching facilities in Arabia. The government encouraged this by giving scholarships and bursaries to suitable candidates, enabling them to attend Egyptian and Syrian schools and later to attend educational institutions in Britain, France, Germany and other countries, including the United States.

In 1930, it seemed likely that some oil companies might be ready to make a substantial down payment for the right to explore eastern Arabia, especially since oil had been found on one of the islands of Bahrain. Saudi Arabia was in need of money to ride out an economic storm until the re-establishment of the pilgrimage on a more profitable basis. The subsequent creation of a government where the Crown Prince serves as Prime Minister and Foreign Minister set a pattern for the future. Yet closer contact with the world, and an almost miraculous discovery of the necessary means to progress, combined in the last decade of the King's reign to create a social and economic revolution that by far surpassed the wildest dreams of those who had seen the early Saudi armies march into Jeddah a little more than a quarter of a century before.

3-1-1 Traditions, Tribes and reform Reactions

To understand government in the Arab Gulf states, one must first have some knowledge of tribal systems and tradition and at least an elementary knowledge of Islam. The relationships between religion, tribalism and the government have changed markedly in the Gulf, particularly since the enormous oil wealth of the 1970s. It is not enough to say that the political systems in the Gulf are based upon tribalism and Islam. Almond and Coleman (1960) observed that "the customs and rhetoric of tribalism and Islam are very prominent and that the institutions in which they are embodied have undergone drastic changes due to the fact that the state provides the individual with many of the benefits that in the past were provided by the tribe. As a result, the economic foundation of Arabian tribalism has ceased to exist".

The balance of power between the central authority and the tribe is now tilted toward the state, and this did not occur by accident. The Gulf governments absorbed all of the institutions of Islam and tribalism into the state and the people of these states are permitted to organise socially and participate politically only through these institutions.

The changes that occurred at the socio-political level were not limited to the almost complete elimination of institutionalised tribalism. King Abd -al Aziz Al Su'ud (Ibn Su'ud), the founder of the modern Kingdom, relied heavily on those trained in religion for advice and administrative support. His potent Saudi military force, originally recruited for religious purposes only, became a powerful political force in the Kingdom in the 1920s, spearheading the Saudi conquest of western Saudi Arabia (Hejaz), including the holy cities of Makkah and Medinah.

With the emergence of a Saudi bureaucracy in the 1950s and 1960s, secularly educated Saudis staffed many of the new offices and provided a set of selected political advisers and administrators who shared their views on government and administration institutions. The Ulama remained an important interest group within the Kingdom. Their voice was, and is still heard by Saudi rulers. In comparison, during the 1950s, the Sultan of Oman faced a challenge to his control from the "Ibadi" Imam. Politics, rather than theological loyalties distinguish the sect from the mainstream of Islamic thinking and practice.

From the beginnings of the twentieth century, the Sultan in Muscat and the Ibadi Imam in Nizwa had a temporary working arrangement that separated their spheres of influence. In the 1950s efforts by the British-backed Sultan to extend his influence, combined with a more aggressive stance taken by the Ibadi Imam, led to armed conflict between the two. The British-led forces of the Sultan put down the Imam's challenges and established direct Omani control over the interior. Since that time, there have been new indications of political opposition in the Sultanate. Omani rulers sought to incorporate Islamic institutions into agencies of the state. The official Ulama thus became an important player in the state's strategies, providing religious sanction to the political order. Religious courts have been placed under the control of the Ministry of Justice, with judges appointed by the state authorities from among religious scholars.

Governments in the Arab Gulf States have established or taken over financial and administrative responsibilities for religious schools and training institutions. The governments designate officials, such as the Grand Mufti of Oman, or committees within their Ministries of Awqaf and religious affairs to issue faatwa (religious judgment) on major issues. In Saudi Arabia, a Ministry of Justice was established in 1970 to supervise the court systems. A committee named "the Directorate of Religious Research, Faatwas, Proselytisation and Guidance", has assumed authoritative religious interpretation.

The influence of this religious phenomenon on the tradition of Gulf politics can also be seen in the relationship between the elites of religious men and the men of power. In the Gulf States, these relationships have historically been close. In the past a local mosque preacher in a middle-sized Arabian city would have been chosen by the local notables, or would have inherited his position from his father or uncle whom he had followed in pursuit of religious education. His salary would come from the local community or from the income generated from *awqaf.* Today, the local mosque is likely to have been built or re-furbished with government funds, and the preacher is likely to be appointed by the state as a salaried employee. Bill (1984) observed that in the decade after the 1973 oil boom, the number of mosques in the Gulf Arab States tripled. While some were privately financed, most mosque construction is being planned and financed by governments. In some states, a mosque is likely to be built with private funds and a preacher hired on an individual basis; examples are the mosques of Kuwait, Bahrain, and Saudi Arabia.

The Ulama in Saudi Arabia have access to the state media for religious instruction and proselytisation and enjoy enormous influence over the content of non-religious writings and programming that fall under state auspices. The highest levels of the Ulama also enjoy direct access to the King for discussion on matters of concern to them. Certain aspects of state social policy, such as the role of women in society and some portions of the educational policy, have been turned over to the Ulama by the government.

There are, of course, a few things that make Saudi Arabia remarkable among Gulf States. Saudi Arabia holds a special place in the Muslim world and the hearts of Muslims since it is home of the holy cities of Makkah and Al-Medinah. The impact of Islam on the political system and the vast oil wealth at the state's disposal have combined to produce a state religious bureaucracy of far greater size and power

40

than those of the other Gulf States. An entire Ministry of the Saudi government is devoted to managing the annual pilgrimage to Makkah, when the Kingdom plays host to more than two million visitors each year.

An anticipated consequence of the development of the vast complex of Saudi religious institutions is the ability of the state to provide jobs for a large number of graduates from religious educational institutions. By providing the Ulama with salaries, social status, positions of political importance and opportunities to spread their message outside the Kingdom, the Saudi state has tried to link the ideological and political interests of the men of religion to the Saudi mechanism of government.

Even though, generally, all Gulf dynasties have been settled in urban areas for at least 200 years, if not longer, they have maintained their historic ties to the nomadic tribes and asserted the right to rule based upon their tribal linkage and Islamic tradition.

The Al Sabah family in Kuwait and the Al Khalifas in Bahrain both established their rule in the late eighteenth century as a consequence of the migration to the coast by segments of the Bani Utab tribe of the Unayza confederation. The Al Nahyan laid clam to Abu Dhabi in the 1760s as the heirs apparent to the Sheikhs of the Bani Yas tribal confederation, some of whose members had moved to the coast from the interior of the Arabian Peninsula. The Al Sa'id of Oman originate from the Abu Sa'id tribe, which has been an
important base of support for them. Their claim to govern the whole of Oman stems from the election of the founder of the state in the 1700s.

All administrative affairs, even those outside religious institutions, were mediated through the Sheikhs. The tribes, however, could easily shift their allegiances either in response to challenges from within the ruler's family or tribal group, or rival claimants. The tribes were difficult to discipline and extract tax revenues from. They could mobilise their own military forces, and if sufficiently provoked, those tribes in some cases, would simply pack up their possessions and move to another jurisdiction. Given this situation, Gulf rulers over the last three centuries have followed a number of strategies to lessen their dependence upon tribal loyalties. They cultivated support from urban populations, some of who still claim tribal affiliations, but can be mobilised on the basis of economic interests and urban

41

solidarity. In the coastal emirates, the rulers came to rely on local merchants, particularly those involved in the pearl trade, for taxes and political support.

British protection was vital to maintaining the smaller emirates of the Gulf coast against the more powerful forces of the Ottoman and Persian empires in the first half of the twentieth century. British support lessened the rulers' need for tax revenues, and gave them the ability to offer the tribes financial inducements for loyalty. Bahrain provides an example of how British intervention altered the relationship between the ruling family and the tribes. Prior to the 1920s, most of the important economic activity on the Island was organised on an exclusively tribal basis. Agricultural land was divided up and administered directly by members of the Al Khalifa family, who ruled mostly *Shi'a* peasants. In the 1920s the tribal courts were abolished and replaced by a centralised court system administered from the capital. The Al Khalifa agricultural estates system was ended with the introduction of private property and laws governing landlord-tenant relations. One-third of the oil revenues accruing to the state were set aside for the ruling family. The right to collect taxes was reserved for the state. Military factions, particularly in the estates, were disbanded and efforts were undertaken to establish a central police force. A municipal council was set up in the capital of Bahrain and the Customary Council, which adjudicated commercial issues, was organised, with the government appointing five of its members. These changes, however, did not occur peacefully. Britain forced the abdication of the ruler, Sheikh Isa, in favour of his son Hamad in 1923 because of Isa's opposition to reform. There were also attacks on Shi'a villages by members of Al Khalifa, who lost control over their estates. Tribes who were hurt by the centralisation of government also carried out attacks. Some of Al Khalifa responsible for the attacks were brought before state courts by the British forces, while others were exiled. In subsequent Bahraini political history, the curbing of tribal and family autonomy did not end tribal and family power; it simply changed the way it was exercised. The office of the ruler and the administrative instruments of his state became dominant. Oil revenues, going directly to the state, increased its power. Once the *Sunni* Arab tribes and ruling family were no longer major threats, the rulers turned to them to staff many important state offices.

Al Khalifa had come to control the political, as opposed to the technocratic, ministries in the government and a number of other bureaucratic positions. The armed forces and police forces were headed by members of the family and recruited largely from Bahrainis with tribal backgrounds. The British reforms in

Bahrain changed the balance of power between the ruler and the previously autonomous groups, but did not break the political alliances holding them together.

The political map of the Arab side of the Gulf, both in terms of state boundaries and ruling dynasties (with the exception of the Saudi), was determined by British policy during the late nineteenth and early twentieth centuries. Britain entered a very fluid tribal and political milieu, where clan and tribal political entities rose and fell and territorial boundaries were both amorphous and fluctuating. Both for their own immediate political purposes, and out of a mistaken belief that these conditions were permanent, the British froze the existing tribal political map. By recognising and protecting some families as rulers in certain territories, they controlled the historical process of political rise and decline and by strengthening the hands of the rulers, they altered the balance of political power domestically. By protecting the smaller states militarily, they halted the expansion of the Saudi state in the first half of the twentieth century. As a result, in the 1960s and 1970s they bequeathed independent sovereign states to the heirs of those ruling families who they controlled. In 1868, the British recognised the Al Thani as the predominant clan in Doha, autonomous from Bahrain and Abu Dhabi, and in 1916 signed a protectorate agreement with them guaranteeing their rule over Qatar.

There are two emirates in the UAE governed by clans from the confederation (Abu Dhabi and Dubai) and two from the Qasimi confederation (Sharjah and Ra's Al-Khayma), as well as other emirates controlled by very small and historically minor tribes. This is not simply the result of tribal factions. Britain, who encouraged these kinds of divisions, came to control not only foreign policy but domestic politics in the smaller emirates as well. Bahrain was the first of the emirates in which Britain took a decisive role in internal affairs and this became a model for subsequent policy elsewhere. British administrators ran what bureaucracy there was. British officers commanded the police and armed forces. British tax collectors collected excise duties. Rulers, who were inconvenient because of excessive independence or
excessive incompetence, were removed from power by Britain. As recently as 1970, a year before the end of their protectorate treaty with Oman, the British engineered the abdication of Sultan Said and the succession of his son Qabus.

With the advent of oil revenues, the rulers in the Gulf States ceased to rely upon local groupings for financial support. Tribal leaders were put on state payrolls, with generous and regular salaries replacing the irregular and less lucrative subsidies of the past. Their ability to provide for their tribesmen was derived from dependence on the state, rather than on their own and/or their tribal resources. Through new state mechanisms, the rulers can appeal directly to tribesmen, without the mediating figure of the Sheikh. Education, medical treatment, subsidised food, housing and state employment are granted directly to the populace, shifting their political focus (if not always their political loyalty) toward the state and away from the tribe. The concentration of education, state employment, and economic activity in major cities drew some Gulf tribesmen out of the desert and into urban life. The most telling sign of the changed political role of the tribes in the Arabian Peninsula is their increasing urbanisation and stability. Saudi Arabia is a good example. By 1970, approximately 10 percent of the Saudi population lived a nomadic lifestyle, as opposed to roughly 40 percent in the 1950s. The oil boom of the 1970s decreased that percentage even further.

Perhaps the best example of the changes that have occurred in the past century in relations between states and tribes in the Gulf is found in Yemen. With oil discovered there only since the 1980s, the Yemeni government has not had the financial resources with which to entice the Yemeni tribes into a subordinate opposition within the political system. Nor has it been able to muster the military capacity to break tribal autonomy in any significant way. As a result, tribal forces in Yemen are still independent and in some cases well armed and important actors in Yemeni politics. Many tribes in Yemen have been able to maintain an independent military. The rulers' efforts to maintain ties with the past and to use historic authority structures to bolster the legitimacy of the rulers are obvious. When the Sultan of Oman makes a yearly tour through the interior and southern parts of the country he receives tribal leaders and local notables. In Kuwait, the only Gulf monarchy with an elected parliament, the government has drawn districts so as to over-represent tribal constituencies. Many of the tribes in primary elections produce the candidates (two in each district) whom the tribe will support. While such elections are not technically permitted under Kuwaiti electoral law they are tolerated, if not encouraged, by the government.
There is an effort to portray rulers as true inheritors of the Arabian tribal traditions. All the Gulf rulers have continued to wear the traditional full-length garment (*thobe*), and head-dress (*kuffiya*). It is interesting to note that the leaders of Yemen and Iraq, who donned western-style suits or military uniforms after their revolutions, are now frequently pictured on official occasions in tribal garb. In Oman, all state employees on official business are required to wear the curved dagger called "*janbiyya*". The exhibit "Saudi Arabia: Yesterday and Today", which toured the United States 1989-1990, emphasised the seamless integration of

tribal traditions, Islam, modern technologies and advanced social services in the Kingdom.

A practice that is common to this approach is Gulf government claims that the Shari'a or Islamic law is the basis of their legal systems and that Islam is the religion of the state. The interpretations of Gulf tribal and Islamic values are obviously accepted by large numbers of the people. These interpretations strike many in their societies as culturally authentic. Tribal heritage and Islam are extremely important in the lives of many of the people of these states. The Gulf dynasties are not appealing to a sentiment foreign to the Islamic and traditional sentiments of those whom they rule.

Tribalism and Islam are important markers of personal and social identity. The institutions of tribalism and Islam have developed into significant supports for the existing political systems in the Gulf dynasties. Political groups and social institutions throughout the Gulf States have called for more regular and formal access to the decision-making progress. Gulf governments have responded with promises of reform and change. The Consultative Council is one aspect of this transformation.

It would be a mistake to assume that there are no impulses from society in the Gulf Arab states for representative and participatory institutions. Demands for a say in decision-making have been mediated through numerous institutions. Some demands are made by traditional social groups such as tribes and religious institutions, which have adapted extremely well to representing the interests of their constituents. Others are more self-consciously modern institutions based on class, function, and ideological interests. Political parties, with both leftist-nationalist and Islamist leanings, have operated in a semi-public way in Kuwait and Bahrain, the two states with some experience in elected assemblies. Though they have never been able to declare themselves formally, Islamic groups such as the Muslim Brotherhood and the Salafi movement on the Sunni side and various Shi'a groups have been increasingly important political actors in many of the Gulf countries. Since 1990, political groups and social institutions throughout the Gulf have increased their political activism. Gulf governments have responded with promises of reform and change, some of which have been carried out. The establishment of the Saudi Majlis Ash Shura comes as an indication of the process of political development and the accommodation of emerging interest in the Kingdom.

Having experienced the relative penury of the pre-oil boom period, Arabs in the Gulf States were delighted to receive employment and benefits from the government. Given the small populations of these countries, a very large portion of the populace saw real improvement in their material condition and they attributed this improvement to their governments.

As the role of the state in these countries grew it attracted interest and activism, the result of which was demands for representative institutions and responsible governments. The demands spring from the very processes of state growth and expansion occasioned by the oil boom. The Gulf States have become the source of economic development, the major employer and the provider of numerous social and other services. It is natural that the people should seek some control over institutions that so powerfully affect their lives, if only to reduce the chance of drastic and unexpected changes in policies. After twenty years of state benefits derived from oil, people have come to regard these benefits as a permanent subsidy from their rulers, and have come to see the benefits as their right. Because of this change in the way the people have started to view things, the Gulf States have taken on more general obligations, hoping to encourage economic growth and safeguard the health of the economy as a whole. On both personal and national levels, people increasingly hold the state accountable for economic conditions. It is the urge to institutionalise that accountability that leads people to demand some role in the political process. It is precisely because the state has become so important and so powerful that people want to participate.

Populations in all Gulf States are increasing while oil prices are fluctuating. The governments have been providing employment opportunities. Bureaucracies are no longer expanding dramatically and measured economic growth has replaced the "black goldrush". As the efficacy of other avenues of political influence and participation has declined, the expansion of the state educational system in the Gulf monarchies, which is funded by oil money, has produced a growing number of people who have the intellectual resources and proclivity to voice their political demands. Those educated generations have been exposed to critical approaches in the analysis of political issues. They have been taught in state curricula to take a country-wide view of their political allegiance and responsibilities, even if these curricula have not encouraged direct political participation.

Although oil wealth did, at the beginning, reduce demands for participation in the early years of the oil boom, or at least gave rulers the resources to divert what demands there were, the processes of state growth and educational expansion led to a new wave of demands from societies in the Arab Gulf dynasties. These demands are the unintentional, but in many ways inevitable, results of state policies pursued over that last two decades. The strength of tribal social structures does not preclude demands by the people for a role in politics. As noted above, some Kuwaiti tribes conduct primary elections to nominate legislative candidates whom the entire tribes support in the general election (a process common in Jordan and Yemen). Islamic groups throughout the Gulf States point to the Kurānic injunction that rulers practice consultation (Shura) in government to support their calls for representative institutions that can act as a check on the arbitrary power of the executive. In Bahrain, the Shi'i social religious institutions called *ma'atim* (these are mostly funerary societies that plan the yearly A'shoor'a celebrations commemorating the martyrdom of Husain) have been an important basis for political organisation. Thus it can be argued that Islam and tribalism are not immutable political facts. They are frameworks of social and individual identity.

It would also be a mistake to assume that the only bases of political organisation in the Gulf States are family, tribal, or sectarian. Other civil society groups (e.g. the Kuwaiti Chamber of Commerce) have been active participants in the policy making process. In Saudi Arabia, the Council of Chamber of Commerce co-ordinates the activities of the nineteen regional chambers. In drafting legislation government ministries consult the various arms of the council. The council and its regional chambers actively lobby the government and the royal family on issues of concern. Some intellectuals have taken to heart the calls for Gulf unity that accompanied the founding of the Gulf Co-operation Council in 1981, calling for the establishment of trans – Gulf institutions. A group of Gulf intellectuals, businessmen and administrators has been meeting yearly since 1979 to discuss economic and social issues.

In 1986, they adopted the name "*muntada al-tanmiyya*", or the Development Forum. The group sometimes broadly addresses political issues, such as participation in the political process, the role of women in society, and the role of the media. In May 1992, in the wake of the Gulf war, ninety Gulf intellectuals, academics, businessmen, and political figures established the Gulf National Forum. That forum was established with the explicit aims of confirming democratic values and political participation, and encouraging the development of "civil society institutions" in the GCC States.

Gulf states witnessed an increase in open political activity in the period after the Iraqi invasion of Kuwait. King Fahd's announcement in November 1990 of plans to institute a consultative assembly (Majlis Ash-Shura) seems to have been taken as an indication that the doors were open for the Saudi people to present their demands in a more organised way. The establishment of Majlis Ash-Shura and announcement of the Basic Law of Government (constitution), the Law of the Council of Ministers and the Law of the Provinces in 1992 facilitate this opening.

In December 1991, 54 prominent Qataris people submitted a petition to the Amir. The petitioners criticized the absence of freedom of expression in the media, confusion surrounding the civil rights of the people and the naturalisation process, a major issue in a country where non-Qataris outnumber Qataris by almost three to one. Their specific recommendation to the ruler was in the area of administration, and not policies. The Amir chose to extend the life of the original appointed body over the past twenty years rather than to permit elections in response to the petition.

In July 1992, a petition signed by over two hundred Bahrainis was submitted to the Amir, calling for the restoration of the National Assembly, which was suspended in 1975 through direct and free elections. The petition stated that an appointed council "to widen the scope of the consultation that the government wants to undertake" would not conflict with the responsibilities of the National Assembly, nor would it take the place of the National Assembly as a constitutional legislative power.

An article appeared in the Arab newspaper *Al Hayat* (October 28, 1991, and December 8, 1992) arguing that no similar petitions had emerged in the UAE or Oman, but the issues in other Gulf States were discussed in both countries, particularly in UAE. *Al-Hayat* (March 2, 1993, p.7) stated that in March 1993, at a public meeting held with members of the UAE Federal National Council, the consultative council appointed by the rules, there were a number of political and intellectual figures who supported the writing of a permanent constitution for the state, an expanded legislative and oversight role for the Federal National Council and direct election of its members.

In states with established constitutions, such as Kuwait and Bahrain, appeals to rulers stress the importance of the constitution as the only acceptable basis of politics. In Qatar, which has a provisional constitution, the demand was for a constituent legislative body that would draw up a permanent constitution. In Saudi

Arabia, both Islamist and liberal petitioner emphasized the importance of implementing Shari'a *or Islamic law.*

Another important and common theme for reform is the need for an institutionalised mechanism for political participation. In Kuwait and Bahrain, which have a history of elected legislative assemblies, demands were for the restoration of those bodies. In Qatar this sentiment was voiced through the request for a new consultative body with more independence and wider powers than the current consultative council. In Saudi Arabia, all three petitions expressed support for the proposed Majlis. In Kuwait, popular demands were not for change, but for a return to the constitutional status. The Kuwaiti state was shaken by the Iraqi invasion and was in desperate need of support from its people. In this regard *Al-Hayat* (March 2, 1992) stated that, given the impact of that invasion, Majlis Al Umma was elected in a very open manner. Government authorities observed strict formal neutrality, though there were persistent rumours that the ruling family members indirectly supported government friendly candidates. The government took the results of the election to heart. Shortly after the polling, the Amir met with ten parliamentarians from various groups and told them that he would meet monthly with the president of the Majlis, his deputy and the heads of the major parliamentary committees. He indirectly pledged not to dissolve this Majlis as he had dissolved the previous one. In its October 13, 1992 edition, *Al Hayat* stated that the Amir consulted deputies on the make-up of the new government. The deputies reaffirmed the Amir's constitutional right to choose the Prime Minister. Some political groups, including the Democratic Forum and the Islamic Constitutional Movement, had advocated during the campaign a formal separation of the offices of Prime Minister and Crown Prince. The fact that the political groups were willing to accept a continued link between the head of government and the Al Sabah family is an indication of the limited nature of their opposition to the Kuwaiti status quo. With this issue resolved, the Amir quickly re-appointed Crown Prince Su'ud Abd - Allah as prime minister. After extensive consultations with deputies, Sa'ad announced his new government on October 17, 1992. In the first year of its term, the new Majlis exhibited a strong tendency toward independence from the government and the assertion of its oversight role. The Leader of Representatives Bloc and speaker of the previous Majlis, Ahmed Al Sa'dun, was an outspoken critic of the government.

It can be argued that the experience of the Gulf states in areas of political participation and representation is new and different in many aspects. First there are no inherent cultural or historical impediments inhibiting the populace from expressing their views on Governmental functions. People are allowed by their respective governments to advance their interests. People can form organisations, tribal groups or Islamic institutions. The traditional institutions have shown remarkable flexibility in adjusting to the circumstances that face large bureaucratic states, modern technologies and drastically changed economies. The growing role of the state in the life of the people over the past twenty years has called forth new demands for political participation and government accountability. As the state has become to mean more in peoples' everyday existence, they naturally want to have some control over its actions. The vast expansion of educational opportunities, funded by the states' oil wealth, has produced a larger body of people able to articulate concerns in abstract and theoretical terms, rather than as personal appeals for individual favors. This in itself is evidence of the success of government reforms since previously personal favouritism often took precedent over commercial interests.

On March 1, 1992 King Fahad of Saudi Arabia announced three Royal Decrees that established three important changes in Saudi domestic political law: a "Basic Law of Government", which is a constitution-like document; "The Statute for a New Majlis As-Shura", and "A System of Regional Government for the Kingdom's Fourteen Provinces". On August 20, 1993, the King issued four more decrees, appointing the members of Majlis Ash-Shura, setting out its rules of operation and amending the character of the Council of Ministers, the Saudi Cabinet.
A clear picture of the Saudi government can be seen through a discussion of certain selected articles from the Basic Law. The Basic Law specifically states that the constitution of the Kingdom is founded on the Kurān and the tradition of prophet Muhammad (Pbuh). It therefore maintains the position that Saudi Arabia, as the Islamic state par excellence, has no need for a formal constitution. The basic system is clearly intended to set out the foundations of the state and the distribution of political power within it. Article 5 asserts that the system of government is monarchical, with rulership resting in the sons and grandsons of King Abd - al Aziz Al-Su'ud, the founder of the modern Kingdom. Article 7 reaffirms Islamic law as the basis of the Kingdom, stating that the government draws its authority from the Kurān and Al Sunna, and that these two sources govern all administrative regulations of the state. The section on rights and duties, Article 23, enjoins the state to protect the principles of Islam, enforce its Shari'a' (laws of Islam), ordain what is good and forbid what is evil (again a Kurānic injunction) and undertake the duty of the call to God. Article 44 defines the powers of the state as the judicial power, the executive power and the power to issue administrative law. The basic

50

system avoids reference to "legislative power". Articles 56, 57, 58 and 60 state that the King is the Prime Minister and Supreme Commander of all military forces. Even though Article 46 defines the judiciary as an independent branch of government, Article 52 states that the King appoints judges and oversees the application of the Islamic Shari'a, the administrative regulations and the general policy of the State. The King has the right to choose the Crown Prince, whose selection had been formerly restricted to informal councils within the state (Article 5). (For a complete version of the Basic Law in English see Appendix III.)

It is through the articles that establish the rights of the Saudi people that the Saudi government has begun to respond to demands voiced in petitions for the rule of law. Articles 33 and 40 guarantee the sanctity of private homes and private communications from intervention or inspection by state authorities, except by due process of law. Articles 27 and 31 oblige the state to provide health care for all Saudi people. Articles 36 and 38 assure freedom from arbitrary arrest and punishment.

Article 8 mandates the equality of all Saudi people under the Shari'a. Article 26 states that the state protects human rights according to the Islamic Shari'a'. The state also guarantees the protection of private property (Article 18). In Article 43 it is mandated that the public audience of the King and the Crown Prince be open to any Saudi person for petition for redress of grievances. Besides this, the basic system contains a number of provisions meant to ensure accountability in dealing with the public treasury. Article 16 states that public funds are sacrosanct. The complete text of the basic system can also be found in *Al Sharq Al-Awsat*, March 2, 1992, pp.4-5.

Amendments to the chapters of the Charter of the Council of Ministers were issued in a royal decree in August 1993. This Royal Decree reaffirms the central role of the council as both the legislative and executive organ of the Saudi government, setting out the policy of the country in all areas in an effort to encourage upward mobility among Saudi technocrats. The decree also sets a four-year limit on the service of any minister in one position, unless the King gives specific permission for an extension of service. (See Appendix IV).

Building on the King's promise of November 1990, Article 68 of the Basic Law mandates establishment of Majlis Ash-Shura. The King issued by royal decree the founding statute of the council that sets the membership of the council at sixty members, not including the president. All members are appointed by the King (Article 3). Details of Majlis Ash-Shura are given below in Chapter 6.

The third statute announced by King Fahad on March 2,1997 addresses the system of regional governments for the Kingdom's fourteen provinces. (See Appendix V). The statute established greater autonomy for the provincial governors over spending and development priorities in their regions and authorised the establishment of provincial consultative councils on the model of the national consultative council. This initiative is viewed by the government as a major effort to decentralise authority in the Kingdom. In September 1993, the King appointed the local councils, twenty-member councils for the major cities of Riyadh, Makkah and Madina. Fifteen-member councils were appointed for the other ten regions. Included in the local councils are the regional representatives of the major government ministries.

These constitutional innovations in the Saudi political system are an attempt to respond to various Saudi constituencies and expression of the process of political development in the country. The petitions discussed earlier have been powerful social trends to which a response from the government was due. Most of what was new in the proposals seemed to come from the liberal agenda which focused on Majlis Ash-Shura administrative devolution and greater local participation. In his speech of March 1, 1999, King Fahad emphasised the central role of Islam and Shari'a in the three royal decrees and in the changes he was announcing. The King also said that the Book of God and the tradition of His Prophet govern everything that the state decrees in these systems of government. The new system for Majlis Ash-Shura is an updating and development of what exists already, the King added.

3-2 The Historical Legitimacy of the Saudi Political System

The legitimacy of this state, or its right to rule, can be explained first on the grounds of the heroic adventures initiated by the early members of the family who brought the city state of Dariya to the Saudi desert. Secondly, that legitimacy is derived from the love and admiration of the Saudi people for the first founders of this Kingdom and for the effort and sacrifice of the state to unite all the regions of this vast Kingdom under the banner of monotheism, justice, love and brotherhood. This is perhaps the single most important aspect of Al - Su'ud legitimacy. Its claim to authority is based unequivocally upon the Islamic revolution of the first Al

- Su'ud ruler who led an army into the deserts of Arabia to restore Islam to primacy and rid the peninsula of polytheism. The Saudi state is defined by its adherence to the immutable characteristics of Islam and to a lesser degree, tribalism. Al Khuli, (1981) argues that tribes in the Kingdom of Saudi Arabia have been providing the Saudi state with military and political support since the time of the first Saudi founders and that the state resorted to the Islamic ideologies to link the various tribes in the peninsula. The relationships between the institutions of religion and tribalism and the government have not changed since the advent of oil wealth in the 1970s. Al Mana (1980) argued that the Saudi rulers have been an embodiment of Arabian tribal values and of Muslim piety. This embodiment has been constant throughout subsequent periods of change that crystalized the relationships between the religious institutions and the Saudi state. Al Sweel and Wright (1993) argued that the state now has turned to provide directly to individual Saudis many of the benefits that in the past came from the tribe. The balance of power between the central authorities and the tribes is now squarely on the side of the former. They also argue that the religious institutions are now much more dependent upon the state than was the case in the past. These changes, which are supportive of the legitimacy of the state, have not been accidental. Owing to economic reasons, the independent powers of the tribes have been curtailed to become part of the general Saudi political system. Doi (1984) argued that, driven by a sense of love and respect for the religion of Islam, the Saudi state has absorbed all local institutions of Islam into the state apparatus. Different versions of tribalism and Islam have provided institutional, legal support and ideological legitimacy to the State. Dawisha (1992) argued that through this new approach the Saudi populace are permitted to organise socially and participate politically. The Saudi state has no monopoly on the political interpretation of Islam. Based on its adherence to the laws and divine commandments of God and continuing tribal support, the Saudi state claims the religious legitimacy of its rule. The origins of this claim date as far back as 1745, when Mohammed Ibn Sau'ud, ruler of Dariya (the central Arabian oasis), formed an alliance with Mohammed Ibn Abd - al Wahhab, a scholar who was preaching a reform of religious practice through a return to the strict interpretations of Islam. The two Imams signed a covenant in which the religious leadership was given to Ibn Abd Al Whab and the political leadership maintained by Ibn Su'ud. The two Imams liberated Muslims in the area of Najd from ignorance, associating partners with God and the domination of superstitions over Islamic values and rituals. Moreover, they established a political entity that has established the roots of the modern Saudi State. According to Meadows (1971), the other source that provides the state with addition means of legitimacy is the support of the tribes for the state's religious interpretation of Islam as a basis for the Saudi state. Both Islamic ideology and tribal support have been the cement that holds the coalition between the people and Saudi rulers together. Not only that, but the Saudi governments achievements in the areas of development generated tremendous support and legitimacy to the system. The state views the Kurān as the constitution under Islamic law. Thus the basic laws in the modern Saudi state perform much the same functions as constitutional guarantees in the West (Meadows, 1971). The topic of legitimacy can also be discussed from an analytical perspective, considering the situations in other neighbouring states. The social and political backgrounds of various Muslim regions in the Arabian peninsula are very much alike and the culture of the tribes in these areas was and still is relatively similar. Whatever conferred the right upon a certain tribe or group of people to govern and rule, can be claimed by other tribes in another desert area as a similar right. In the past, the whole region shared a difficult economic situation. Such difficult social and environmental living conditions forced the Arab tribes into a unique stream of social, religious and political traditions and affiliations. The head of the tribe is respected and honoured, for he is the provider during times of drought or calamity and the protector against any looming danger. This means that the tribe owes its continued existence, in some respect, to the wise guidance of its chieftain. This dominant role of the tribe that was prevalent in all the Gulf countries has changed not only in Saudi Arabia, as shown earlier, but in other Gulf states as well. That change made room for the belief that an Islamic state is committed to the main cause of the populace, providing for their welfare and encouraging social cohesiveness and consequently for their unity within a unified social and political entity. The Holy Book the Kurān exhorts Muslims to respect, accept and obey their rulers as long as they govern the country in accordance with the laws of Islam (the Shari'a) and do not spread immoral practices that are in contradiction with the commandments of God. The basic principles of Islam, as long as they are observed and practised by a Muslim ruler, can primarily justify the legitimacy of the ruler to govern a Muslim society. Secondly, they are seen to represent a comprehensive method of ruling that can provide for the spiritual and material needs of the populace. The reason Shari'a is viewed as the perfect method is because God revealed it to Prophet Muhammad (Pbuh). This should be a valid reason to support its divine characteristics. Based on this analysis it can be argued that the most important features of the Arab traditional political systems are the prevalence of Islamic values and the way they are observed and practised by the state. According to Al Rashid (1976), the laws of Islam, on the basis of which any true Muslim country is run and administered, are derived from two infallible sources: The Holy Book and the traditions of Prophet Muhammad (Pbuh). The Kurān dictates that Muslims in a Muslim state should live by the commandment of God; and that they are governed by a righteous Muslim leader. The legitimacy of the leader is automatically gained and justified as long as the laws of Islam are protected, exercised and observed by the government. The role of religion, in this case, is to unify Muslims within the boundaries of the creed of Islam and to unify them within one sound society and in the crucible of justice, equality and brotherhood. In regard to the historical legitimacy of the Saudi state, Kinnedy (1987) argued that the short reign of Turki Ibn Abd - Allah had been of the utmost importance in restoring something of the shattered fortunes of the Saudi state and the prestige of the house of Sau'ud. Through strong adherence to Islamic belief, he could at least repair the foundations on which both state and state had risen during the half-century preceding the disaster of Dariya. Kinnedy (1987) also argued that there would be ups and downs in the process of restoration and development. It is fair to say, however, that had it not been for Turki's patient and persistent efforts, empowered by Islamic traditions, which guided him through the repair of the ruin he inherited, the Saudi Arabia of his great-grandson's dreams would never have been realised.

Based on the analysis of the religious reasons that justify the legitimacy of Saudi rule, and in addition to the historical discussions of the heroic struggle exerted by Saudi rulers, it can be argued that the roots of this legitimacy go as far back as the year 1745, which marks the alliance that took place between the ruler and the religious reformer. This legitimacy has been growing and has been enforced and consolidated by successive political, legal, social and educational reforms.

The achievement realised in modern Saudi society can attest to the authenticity of this legitimacy and can equally claim that the Saudi state has employed all its resources to the best interests of the Saudi people.

In modern Saudi society, the process of change and development has been taking place rapidly. However, while one eye is on the traditional Islamic principles, the other is on the proper means of development, so that a bright future for future Saudi generations can be realised. Throughout this process, it can easily be noticed that the traditional form of morality and sound Islamic principles were maintained. The present political system has been functioning to represent the ideal form of government as defined by the laws of the religion of Islam. In this regard Al-Awa (1989) argues that in the Saudi form of government, a strong religious sense is intertwined with any activity carried out by a Saudi official. The strong religious conscience of the public is always active and supervises all that commands virtue and abhors vice. In the Islamic method of government, there is no legislative authority because the legislation in the Kurān is the best legislation possible. Islam allows room for judicial and executive authorities

3-3 The Religious Legitimacy of the Saudi Political System

The Divine Laws in Islam designate appropriate terms to replace secular terminologies such a "political parties", "parliaments" and other political institutions. Islam provides terminologies such as *Majlis Ash-Shura* "consultation council", "Council of the" (Umma), or a council that represents the public (People's Council). Underlying this religion-related structure, the whole Muslim community can be represented by councils characterised by being Islamic in practice, methodology and representation. Any unanimous opinion or decision adopted by these councils is imperative and should be observed by Muslim rulers.

Saudi Arabia has maintained Shari'a law (Divine Law) by adhering to this religious ideological approach. In Saudi society, aspects of social life are completely influenced and affected by the laws and teachings of Islam, which are, in essence, the laws and commandments of God. Hobday (1978) argued that the Kurān is remarkable for the amount of ground it covers in relation to everyday life. It is the most complete of documents setting out not only the religious acts that must be performed, but also seeking to create a society in which every act, social, political, and economic, is governed by the divine law. Conservatism with strict adherence to the laws of God continues to be a major force in the Kingdom. The momentum of conservative opinion continues to grow as a power that derives its legitimacy and energy from the sound principles that were revealed by the Kurān and Sunna. This growth became magnified as the base of economic change increased. According to Al Qassimi, (1990) conservatives and modernists differed in opinion regarding what kind of technology might be appropriately used and how to make best use of the Kingdom's great wealth. The dichotomy between the two is found at the core of much of the Country's political affairs. The unanimous accord of Saudi Muslim scholars, however, states that any process of modernisation should reflect Islamic texture and values. In an article published by El Bilad News paper (1941) King Abd - Al Aziz is quoted, saying:

> "We are proud because we observe Islam. Peace can never be maintained without the strict adherence to Islam. By defending Islam, we are in fact defending our own integrity and peace; its loss will be a total loss for us. Without Islam

we shall be worthy of the wrath of God. What I want and ask from you is to uphold the principles of our religion. This is my policy which I am determined to pursue and I shall not depart from it no matter how great the sacrifice shall be".

The laws of Islam have been observed and respected in the highest rank of office; they are deeply entrenched in the tradition of the State.

It can be argued that the legitimacy of the Saudi state is based on the following factors:

1) The Religious factor. As heard from a Saudi citizen: "We are proud because we observe Islam and peace can never be maintained without the strict adherence to Islam". There is a sense of adherence to the immutable characteristics of Islam. This approach has been strongly welcomed by the tribes in the Arabian peninsula. Present Saudi rulers have adopted this religious spirit.

2) The advent of oil changed the traditional relationships between the institution of religion and the government. The state acted as an embodiment of Arabian tribal values as well. It provided many of the benefits that previously came from the tribe directly to individuals. Due to growing legitimacy, the balance of power between the central authorities (the Saudi rulers) and the tribes has become squarely on the side of the former.

3) As a result of certain economic and tribal-related changes, the religious institutions have become much more dependent upon the state. It follows that religious leaders in the Kingdom now fully support the state. Besides, the independent power of the tribes were located, curtailed and brought into the general Saudi political system. The State has absorbed all local institutions of Islam into the state apparatus by force of its love and respect for religion. As far as legitimacy from a historical perspective is concerned, it can be argued that the origins of that legitimacy date back to 1745, when Muhammad Ibn Su'ud, ruler of *Dariya*, formed an alliance with the pious scholar Muhammad Ibn Abd - al Wahhab, who preached a reform of religious practice through a return to the true path of Islam.

4) The struggle, and chain of sacrifices exhorted by the Saudi State justify their right to rule and their right to preserve the noble purpose of providing the people of the Peninsula with means of secure social and political life. The discussions of the

expeditions and other adventures conducted by early Saudi rulers (e.g. Faisal), attest to the authenticity of this claim.

5) The range of support and loyalty that has been extended to the Saudi rulers by leaders of other Gulf States is discussed to show the legality and justice of the struggle initiated by Saudi rulers to realise peace and brotherhood among tribes. Saudi rulers succeeded in bringing Saudi society from dissension to a modern society.

6) During the past twenty years, the Kingdom of Saudi Arabia has been highly developed in the fields of education, health, industry, agriculture and rural development. The achievements of the Kingdom in these fields are by no means less than the achievements of any Western European State.

Chapter Four:

The Structure of Saudi Government

4-1 Background and Evaluation

The process of change and development in Saudi Arabia has affected the country both socially and politically. This development was financed by oil industry wealth utilised to modernise the Saudi infrastructure and ultimately the way Saudi citizens live. Such progress has been realised with a clear adherence to the laws of Islam as stipulated in the Kurān and the traditions of Prophet Muhammad (Pbuh).

This Islamic approach to development, coupled with significant investment in domestic projects, enabled the government to realise its desire to transform Saudi Arabia from an ancient society to a modern state.

As discussed in previous chapters, Saudi Arabia was in desperate need of a stable and well structured government. Upon uniting the regions that comprise the Kingdom into one polity, it was discovered that the people were suffering from illiteracy and many were living in abject poverty. Saudi rulers themselves are true believers in God and in the religion of Islam. They strongly and sincerely believe that the laws of Islam are the best mechanism through which to rule and this is especially desirable in a region that witnessed the birth of Islam. Since Islam requires all believers to perform the Hajj at least once in a lifetime, as one of the basic pillars in the religion of Islam, Saudi Arabia hosts millions of Muslims each year. This has created an affinity for Saudi Arabia in the hearts of Muslims worldwide. It causes Muslims, even those not from Saudi Arabia, to be careful watchers of the affairs of Saudi Arabia including its policies and implementation of the laws that govern and direct the progress of the state. Political and social developments could not have been easily accomplished or maintained had they not been established through and upon Islamic principles, considering that the initial momentum of the Saudi expansion and unification was founded in a determination to eliminate inequality and put an end to tyranny. The Saudi emphasis on moral government and reform was an offshoot of the alliance between the religious Wahhabi movement and the people.

59

The modern political system in the Kingdom of Saudi Arabia has been designed and shaped in accordance with Islamic ideology, and any separation between the state and religion is absolutely impossible. In this regard, Nyep (1984) argued that Saudi society in the early 1980's, by comparison, represented a marked contrast between the impoverished, largely isolated, and underdeveloped nation formed scarcely 50 years earlier. He also states that the Arabian Peninsula of the early twentieth century was one of the most backward regions of the Middle East. There were a few modern schools with a secular curriculum in the cities of the Hejaz, while the pilgrimage centers of Mecca and Medina attracted devout Muslims and scholars from throughout the Muslim world. From a social perspective, the Arab peninsula was the home of bedouin, nomads and oasis farmers, and the few towns and cities that existed were the domain of merchants who exercised sometimes remote, but effective control over the region. Fisher (1969) observed that tribal loyalties were paramount and political organization was a shifting pattern of alliances that were inherently unstable, and the process of raiding and feuding among the fractious tribesmen was unending and sometimes violent. These circumstances were the primary challenges facing government as it sought to unify the tribes of the Penninsula and implement reforms.

Tribal feuds, raids, and wars instigated against Turks, poverty, famine and natural disasters all demanded a planned framework for social and political developments. In this regard, Holden and Johns (1981) argued that Abd - al Aziz Ibn Abd - al Rahman skillfully manipulated tribal conditions and launched a call for reform in order to weld the refractory bedouins and villagers of Arabia into a modern state. Tribes used to be headed by Sheikhs who represented the political and social leadership, with all activities of daily life revolving around their personalities. The identifiable qualities of leadership being courage, shrewdness, intelligence, prudence, generosity and wealth. Respect was extended to him due to these qualities.

In the settled areas known as emirates, Amirs could maintain their authority owing to the services they extended. The royal State started with an additional responsibility, which was to provide alternatives to the primitive social practices that were prevalent.

According to Willard (1980), it was the traditions that were respected and prevalent throughout the Arab Peninsula that facilitated the peaceful transfer of power from the King to the Crown Prince, and then to other princes.

Regional rulers were ordered by the central government in Aoaina (the birth place of Mohammed Ibn Abd - al Wahhab, the founder of the reform movement and co-founder of the state) to pay an annual allowance of victuals and cash. These allowances were not regarded as tribute, but were rather to insure the right of the merchants of the coastal area to trade with the merchants and people of the hinterland and to insure protection from transgression. This was part of the tradition upon which they organized a system whereby taxes could be collected to support the state. This new system was principally rooted in Kurān. Allah says:

> "The ruler who believes in one God and works as well, shall
> have the Kingdom of the country and its people; for good is
> the divine unity which has been proclaimed by all the
> prophets."

Based on this Kurānic principle, the state is entitled to certain revenues on the earnings of its citizens that are derived from agriculture and trade. One-fifth of all the spoils of war were the predetermined percentage that belonged to the ruler and the preacher Mohammed Ibn Abd - al Wahhab for personal maintenance, and to make possible the performance of their respective duties. The ruler and the preacher acted as a single entity with dual functions. Half a century of such harmonious co-operation has few equivalents.

When the growth of the state began to lay excessive burdens on the Sheikh, it was he who transferred the executive responsibility for political and financial administration to the King. The King continued to consult him on all matters. This relationship laid the foundation for and was perhaps the first example of Islamically established Shura, used as a method of government in the Arabian Peninsula. Since that time this religion-based principle of consultation has been firmly adopted as a method in the administration of the modern state. Taxes were paid regularly under the threat of substantial fines in the event of delay or evasion. The King's calls on the towns and tribes for the amounts to that the state was entitled in connection with its military activities were generally met promptly and in full.

A fee of no more than five pounds per pilgrim was imposed on pilgrims making the Hajj during the days when the pound sterling was on the gold standard.

The payment of fees in gold, or its market equivalent, certainly had the appearance, from the point of view of the pilgrims, of greatly increasing their burden, even though this change had occurred throughout the world. The pilgrim fees were eventually completely abolished by order of the King, as government resources from oil and other sources eliminated the need for the fees. The government assumed the entire cost of ever-increasing amenities. For instance, tarmac roads with several traffic lanes were built from Mecca to Mt. Arafat to benefit all pilgrims.

Another example and benefit of the harmony that existed within the unified Kingdom was the co-operation between the regional rulers and Saudi rulers. One example was the incident where Mohammed Ibn Rashid, Sheikh of Ha'ail, answered Abd - Allah Ibn Faisal's call for help. This happened in 1885 at the beginning of the second Saudi State. This incident is also indicative of the role tribal leaders played, bolstering the legitimacy of the Al - Su'ud state. The modern state of Saudi Arabia was crowned by the achievements of Abd - al Aziz Ibn Su'ud, though what characterizes this era is the range of socio-political reforms.

4-2 Integrated Building of the Government

By 1932, most regions of the Arabian Peninsula had begun an era marked by political and social change. During the reign of King Abd - al Aziz, which began in 1932, a limited administrative government functioned in Saudi Arabia. It comprised affiliated organs such as the Royal Court, the Judiciary Department, Internal Security, Defence and Treasury. With the advent of affluence arising from oil, the Saudi state found itself well placed to improve the economic and social standards of the people. Schools were built, roads were constructed and the Post Telegraph and Telephone (PTT) was introduced and later improved. Departments of the government were established to oversee agriculture, commerce, and civil aviation through which the rights of the people to public services were realized. Prior to 1950, only three ministries were in existence, Foreign Affairs, Finance and Defence. A number of other government departments were working, but within limits not imposed upon the others. Soon the government began to co-ordinate the responsibilities of those departments, and eventually these services were entrusted to a single department. Similar departments were grouped into ministries. In the early stages Saudi Arabia consisted of four major emirates: Najd, Al-Ahsa, Hejaz and Asir. These emirates constituted the nucleus of the Saudi realm. Each emirate maintained its own distinct character.

The administrative functions in each emirate were limited to providing basic services and maintaining peace, law, and order.

In a publication sponsored by the Ministry of Finance and National Economy, (1971) it is stated that during the early stages of the formation of the Saudi government only two offices of public administration were active: one was in the Hejaz area, and the other looked after the affairs of the rest of the Kingdom. In the same publication it is stated that under the administrative system of government that was enacted in 1926, the formation of the following directorates was mandated:

1. International Affairs: the Directorates of Public Security, Health, Public Telephone and Telegram (PTT) and Municipalities.
2. The Directorate of Finance.
3. The Directorate of Education.
4. Shari'a Affairs: The Departments of the Judiciary, Pilgrims and Endowments, and the Holy Mosque.
5. The Audit Bureau.
6. The Consultation Council (to be discussed in a separate chapter)
7. The Directorate of Military Affairs.
8. The Directorate of Foreign Affairs.
9. The Directorate of General Inspection.

The last three of these directorates were directly affiliated and attached to His Majesty the King. The remaining was attached to the office of the King's Deputy in Hejaz. From a social and administrative perspective, the State relied on tribal organisation, and tribal councils ran the rest of the Kingdom in the initial stage of the amir system.

With the passage of time, some of these directorates were changed into ministries. For example, the Ministry of Foreign Affairs was established in 1930, the Ministry of Defence in 1944, and the Ministry of Finance in 1932. As resources increased, government expanded and of course the number of public officials increased. The Ministry of Health was established in 1951 and the Ministries of Education, Agriculture and Commerce were established in 1952. The need for greater centralization, aimed at better coordinating the activities of the already established ministries, necessitated that the Council of Ministers be established. A Royal

Decree to that effect (No. 4288) was enacted. This Royal Decree signalled the true beginning of modern government administration in the Saudi Kingdom. In order to modernise its administrative system, the government hired experts who provided technical assistance from the International Monetary Fund (IMF) and took steps based on the recommendations and advice of these experts. In order to improve the performance of the government administrative mechanism, the King requested assistance from the United Nations from 1958 to 1960. Reforms resulted in a remarkable change that yielded an increase in both the government budget, and the number of government employees from 22,217 to 31,097 during the same period.

As the financial resources of the Saudi government increased, the objectives of the Council of Ministers began to plan programs to address less obvious needs and goals; regulatory measures were issued by the Council in 1963.

The public administrative structure of the Saudi government can be divided into three categories: (1) the central administration, (2) the regional and local administration and (3) the municipal administration.

The Council of Ministers, as established in 1953, has become a legislative and executive authority. It was and still is the most authoritative body in the Kingdom. It is within its jurisdiction to formulate government policy on internal and foreign affairs. Of all the agencies and organised bodies of the government, the Council of Ministers is the most influential. It derives its power directly from the King, and it can examine almost any matter in the Kingdom. The Council of Ministers holds regular weekly meetings. Its decisions do not come into effect unless they are approved by the King in his capacity as Prime Minister. Despite its relatively recent origins, the Saudi Council of Ministers emerged in 1953 as the natural political outcome of Abd - al Aziz Bin Su'ud's final consolidation of power and his unification of the Kingdom. King Abd - al Aziz established two major bodies, to govern the affairs of the Hejaz and the Western province. The first body, which still exists, was the Consultative Council (Majlis Ash-Shura). A second body, created later, was the Council of Deputies, which in 1953 evolved into the Council of Ministers. The Council of Deputies derived its authority directly from the King and was able to issue direct instructions to other government bodies and agencies.

The Council oversees such affairs as domestic and foreign polices, the approval of the annual budget, the making of new appropriations, the approval of international treaties and agreements, the appointment or dismissal of high officials, the examination of draft regulations prepared by the consultation council and the amendment or rejection of proposed laws. Its authority and duties are specified within the Regulatory Law issued in 1954.

Prior to the departure of late King Abd - al Aziz in 1953, the number of Ministries was nine, and later increased to twelve. Three additional ministries were added during the reign of King Su'ud and two ministries were established during the reign of King Faisal.

In the early 1940s, having achieved its immediate goals, the Council of Deputies began to decline, while the Central Government began to exercise a wider authority over the country and began to provide more services at both the national and local levels. With the expansion of the area centrally administered and of services provided by the central government, new ministries and departments had to be established. In 1951, the jurisdiction of the Minister of the Interior was extended to the whole of the nation, functioning as an agency of the Interior rather than as a Ministry.

Organisational Chart of Council of Ministers

Prime Minister (The King)	
Deputy Premier Crown Prince	Experts Division
Ministry of Foreign Affairs	Presidency Cabinet of Council of Ministers
Ministry of Justice	General Secretariat for Council of Ministers
Ministry of Pilgrimage	Ministry of Defence And Aviation
Ministry of Information	Ministry of Interior
Ministry of Public Works and Housing	Ministry of Labour and Social Affairs
Ministry of PTT	Ministry of Finance and National Economy
Ministry of Planning	Ministry of Health
Ministry of Higher Education	Ministry of Transport
Ministry of Municipalities and Rural Affairs	Ministry of Education
Ministry of Water	Ministry of Agriculture
Ministry of Industry and Electricity	Ministry of Commerce
Ministry of Islamic Affairs, Endowments and Preaching	Ministry of Civil Service

The structure of regional governments and the composition of the regional governing bodies and regional councils provide further evidence of the government's desire to increase the involvement of the people in government affairs, while at the same time maintaining stability. These measures were not cautious attempts to move towards Western-style democratic institutions. Rather, they were seen as logical and sensible extensions of the traditional participative mechanisms that have facilitated good government in the Kingdom and have allowed the inevitable pressures of rapid growth to be resolved through the emergence of a broad-based consensus.

The basic system, which incorporates the arrangement of Majlis Ash-Shura and regional government, was established in written form both as a description of the essential structure and organisation of government and as a bill of rights for the citizen (Appendix III). Article 1 established the basic tenets of the Kingdom, stating that: "The Kingdom of Saudi Arabia is an Arab and Islamic Sovereign State; its religion is Islam and its constitution is the Holy Kurān and the Prophet's tradition". Article 5 says the form of the government is "monarchical." Article 7 states that: "Rule in the Kingdom depends upon and must confirm to the teachings of Islam," while Article 8 provides justice, consultation and equality in accordance with the Islamic Shari'a.

These basic tenets define the responsibilities of the state in some detail, giving special reference to the Kingdom's duties as guardian of the Holy places and setting guidelines for the exploitation of the state's wealth to ensure the economic and social development of the Kingdom. The people's rights to security, to self-fulfilment through education and freedom of opportunity and to the ownership of property are all safeguarded. A right to privacy is also guaranteed.

Organizational Chart : Kingdom of Saudi Arabia

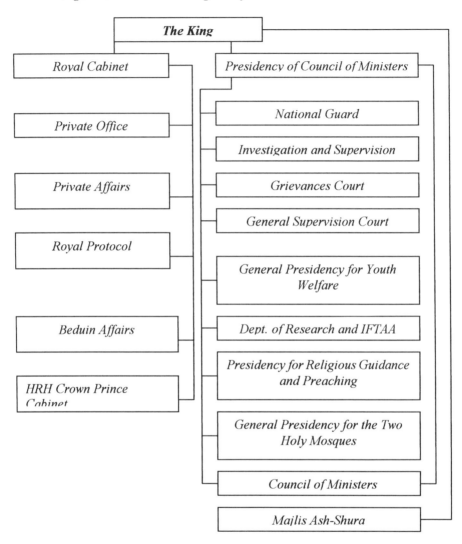

The Articles set out with remarkable clarity the principles upon which the Kingdom is governed and the rights and obligations of both the state and the citizen. As the processes of consultation were extended, it became necessary to formalise the principles underlying the traditions. This enabled the Kingdom to pass through periods of extraordinary progress with an equally extraordinary degree of stability. The promulgation of the basic laws, the formation of the consultative council and the restructuring of the Kingdom's regional governments are part of this necessary progress.

4-3 Regional and Local Administration

An Amir who is appointed by the King administers each area of Saudi Arabia. Local officials and administrators are subordinate to the Amir. It was not until 1963 that local administrations were formally institutionalised. The Saudi realm was divided into emirates governed by local Amirs who hold ministerial status and act as representatives of the King. The emirates are connected to the central government through the Ministry of Interior. The responsibilities of the Amir include receiving petitions from people in his Majlis and maintaining peace and security within his emirate, while overseeing the activities of the government agencies and municipal officials within it. Article 17 of the ordinance of the Deputies Council, issued in 1932, states that the municipalities in the Western region should be kept under the authority of the Ministry of the Interior, while others are left to be supervised by the regional governors, or Amirs. It also mandates that municipalities should secure their revenues from fees charged on services and finance their expenditures with the help of grants from the government. The Ordinance of 1936 is vital and effective, since it sets the strategy, the policy and the kind of administrative organisation upon which all Saudi cities can be developed into modern municipalities. This ordinance was put into effect from 1936 to 1977.

In 1960 the Municipal Administration was established under the auspices of the Ministry of Interior. In 1962 the Council of Ministers approved the establishment of an independent control system in the Ministry of Interior to deal with municipalities. This sub-ministry was named the Deputy Ministry of the Interior for Municipal Affairs.

The overall organisational structure of government in Saudi Arabia evolved during the nation-building stage, which extended up to the year 1970.

This evolution is attributed to the firm determination of the government to complete the establishment of agencies that could be held responsible for the preparation of future development plans, the implementation of recommendations offered by World Bank experts, the United Nations Technical Co-operation Administration and the Ford Foundation.

The first five-year plan for economic and social development (1970-1975) was prepared by the Central Planning Organisation (now called the Ministry of Planning) in co-operation with the Stanford Research Institute. This was followed by successive five-year plans: 1975-1980, 1980-1985 and 1985-1990. The Kingdom has completed a comprehensive organisational structure outlined as follows: The executive and legislative body is represented in the Council of Ministers. Twenty Ministries have been established along with twelve government agencies, fourteen regional municipalities, six municipalities in major cities, one hundred municipalities of different classes; forty five rural compounds to provide services for rural areas and three agencies for central control. There are thirty-two public corporations, which includes seven universities. There are five independent agencies and six agencies for administrative development.
Classified by their function, the ministries are divided into three sectors:
1.   The Sovereign Affairs Sector includes the Ministries of Foreign Affairs, Defence and Aviation, the Interior and the Presidency of the National Guard.
2.   The Service Sector includes the Ministries of Education, Higher Education, Communication, PTT, Public Works and Housing, Labour and Social Affairs, Pilgrimage and Endowment, Information and Municipal and Rural Affairs.
3.   The Development Sector includes the Ministries of Finance and National Economy, Commerce, Planning, Industry and Electricity, Oil and Mineral Resources and Agriculture and Water. In order to render proper services to the people, most ministries and government agencies have regional branches.
       There are local administration agencies whose task is to assist the central government departments in providing services designed to serve the basic welfare of the people. These agencies supervise the provision of all municipal services such as the implementation of plans approved by the authorities to maintain cities in a clean and beautiful state, along with the delivery of basic services, the protection of the environment and public health and the management of municipal projects.

In spite of the degree of progress and developments that have been achieved in Saudi Arabia, the government felt a need to do more. However, the additional programs that were introduced were not sufficient, since they were not planned or designed using scientific methods. International assistance was requested from experts from various fields, and they provided development-related solutions. Their recommendations were thoroughly studied by the Saudi Cabinet. Consequently the Ministry of Finance was authorised to take any necessary measures to facilitate the implementation of suggested recommendations. Later, a number of domestic administrative and planning agencies and institutes were founded. Among them are the Institute of Public Administration (1961), the Supreme Committee for Administrative Reform headed by the King (1963) and the Central Planning Organisation founded in 1964 and headed by an official of ministerial rank and staffed by selected specialists. This organisation co-ordinates the activities of the other Ministries and national organisations. It oversees the implementation of all development plans initiated by the government. In 1975 this organisation was converted into the Ministry of Planning. An official of ministerial rank undertook the development of an advanced manpower force and heads the General Personnel Bureau. In 1977, its title was changed to the Council of the Civil Service, for planning and the supervision of civil service regulations.

Methodologically speaking, of the government administrative body suffered obstacles that have been too difficult to overcome. Development plans that were proposed faced problems of an organisational nature, such as duplication of activities and services. This resulted in an over expansion of jobs and a huge increase in the cost of government projects and civil services. Lassitude at the administrative level resulted in an inability to cope with the pace of rapid development. Competent utilisation of modern technology was needed to cope with demands for more efficient services. There has been an under-utilisation of the abilities of qualified personnel due to bureaucratic procedures and excessive centralisation of authority. In short, the pace of development has exceeded the ability and talent of the public administration agencies to catch up and adapt to the new challenges and changes. Besides, the behaviour of the employees have been characterised as irresponsible, which in turn influenced the achievements and progress of the agencies where they were employed. The behaviour of the majority of the employees was motivated by the acquisition of personal goods. Favouritism played a clear role in hindering the progress of the various government administrations and this necessitated reform efforts designed and planned on sound ethics. In 1956 the government solicited technical assistance to improve the organisation of its financial strategies and to obtain proposals for and solutions to its administrative problems. The chosen solution, which was unanimously approved by international experts, was to invest in the education of the general public. This resulted in the formation of the Supreme Council for Administrations Reform and the Civil Service Council. The new programs for development were based on scientific principles and experience that proved to be successful. The new reform program was initiated through Royal Decree No. A/90 of 1992. In support of A/90, on August 27, 1992 a Royal Decree was issued to the effect that a Majlis Ash-Shura should be instituted. This was followed by another decree that stipulated the rules that would guide the activities of the Majlis.

Chapter Five:

Ash Shura in the Saudi Political System

5-1 *Ash Shura* in Islam

Ash-Shura (Consultation) is one of the most important elements of the Islamic political system. The Kurān stipulates that it should be applied in the political and personal lives of Muslims. It is obligatory for the individual Muslim ruler to apply this principle, although methods of application are left open, allowing for the consideration of specific circumstances and situations. Ash-Shura is also one of the most important aspects of Islamic political theory. The Kingdom of Saudi Arabia has been following this principle, utilising different methods and degrees of implementation. The most recent of which was the establishment of Majlis Ash-Shura, or Consultative Council, the Kingdom's most prominent political institution. This council assumes several important roles of which the most significant are the enactment of laws and advising the King.

The Importance of *Ash-Shura*

Arabs prior to Islam used the word "Ash-Shura" frequently. Arab language dictionaries contain several definitions of the word and its derivatives. The word Ash-Shura is the infinitive of the verb "*Shawara*", or "consulted". "*Shawartahu*" means "I solicited his advice and consultation." It also means "appearance and extraction."

Idiomatically speaking, the definitions of the word are very close to the literal ones. One definition is "seeking the advice and consultation of scholars and informed people in the affairs that concern the nation and its interests". Ash-Shura has also been defined as "decision-making in the light of the opinions of the concerned parties in the country."

The working definition employed here is "the exchange of viewpoints and opinions with others to formulate together an authentic opinion". Such an opinion will not be authentic unless it agrees with the core of religion, does not contradict a Kurān text and serves the national interest. In light of this definition, Ash-Shura

suggests that one should not be opinionated or obstinate. Instead, one should seek the best and most authentic opinion. Ash-Shura includes three elements:
1.   The person consulting (who seeks others' opinions).
2.   The subject in question.
3.   The advisor (who provides the advice).

Numerous scholars of religion and politics have studied Islamic government and political theory and are almost unanimous in the belief that Ash-Shura is one of the most important political principles in Islam. Further, it represents the general framework within which the Islamic ruling authorities, legislative, executive and judiciary, must act. It excludes obstinacy and stubbornness, helps draw accurate conclusions, realises the unity of the nation, and harmonises the hearts of its people.

Ash-Shura is one of the sources of Shari'a (Divine Law) and a fundamental support in the Islamic political system. The right it confers to the people to participate in government affairs reflects its significance. It also facilitates the enactment of regulations and rules in grey areas, or areas where there is no clear guidance from the Kurān or hadith. No legal case or precedent controls either the interpretation, development, or application of law or principle in such circumstances.

Ash-Shura prevents, in most cases, government violation of laws and abuse of power, since the decision taken by the ruling authorities cannot be implemented unless they were arrived at through this process.

Ash-Shura benefits a nation in the following ways:
1.   It directs polities toward a joint activity between the ruler and his people and establishes strong relations between them.
2.   It leads to political co-operation between the nation and its rulers, allowing the government access to the influence, expertise, knowledge and capabilities of its citizens.

There is consensus among Muslim scholars of Islamic jurisprudence, or Fiqh that Ash-Shura is an obligation, meaning that the ruler must consult the nation regarding general affairs. Shari'a denies legitimacy to any Muslim government that does not render decisions based on Ash-Shura.

The Kurān obliges Muslims to abide by its precepts, so no action will be taken prior to consultation.

The importance of Ash-Shura and its primacy in Islam is also a matter of due process in an Islamic legal system. Prophet Muhammad (Pbuh) emphasised Ash Shura and practiced it. He rendered a very visible and substantial aspect of his Sunna, which also obligates Muslims to its practice since following Al Sunna of the Prophet, who interpreted and implemented the Kurān in his life to a perfect degree, is also an obligation. The companions of the Prophet and the orthodox Caliphs, or rulers, who succeeded the Prophet, acted according to this principle and followed its course in all of their affairs. Islamic history is laden with examples of Ash-Shura carried out in various forms and at different levels. The following is the Kurānic verse that addresses the principle of Ash-Shura:

> It is part of the mercy of Allah that thou dost deal gently with them. Were thou severe or harsh hearted, they would have broken away from about thee: so pass over their faults and ask for Allah's forgiveness for them; and consult them in affairs of the moment. Then when thou have taken a decision, put thy trust in Allah. For Allah loves those who put their trust in him". (*The Holy Kurān, Surah Al-Imran* Verse 159.)

This Kurān verse makes it clear that Ash-Shura is an obligation, since God ordered the Prophet Muhammad (Pbuh) to consult his companions in all matters.
In a chapter named Ash-Shura, in the Holy Kurān, the following words appear in one of its verses that describe "the good Muslim" and stress the importance of abiding by the Ash-Shura principle.

> Those who respond to their lord, and maintain regular prayer, and mutual consultation; who spend out of what we bestow on them for sustenance. (*The Holy Quran Ash-Shura, Verse 38.)*

Ash-Shura, in Islam, did not emerge as a result of the conditions of the society in which Prophet Muhammad (Pbuh) lived. In the view of Muslims, the practice of Ash Shurah is rooted in the Divine ordinances of the Kurān revealed to Prophet Muhammad (Pbuh) and aims at establishing a righteous and stable society. During the era of the Prophet Muhammad (Pbuh), Ash-Shura could be classified into two categories:

1. Ash-Shura practiced at the request of the Prophet, i.e. the Prophet (Pbuh) solicited the advice of the people.

2. Ash-Shura initiated, without his request, by some of his companions. Examples of each category are abundant.

Prophet Muhammad (Pbuh) consulted his companions in times of peace and of war. He consulted them when concluding treaties and agreements with his

75

rivals and when encamping. He was quoted as saying: "People, advise me" on many occasions. Sometimes he would take a decision he deemed necessary to serve the Muslim interest, but when he consulted his companions and realised how powerful and logical their arguments were, he changed his mind and did not act according to his own preferences. His sayings in this regard included, but are not limited to: "The advisor is trusted", "People who consult with each other will be guided to the best conclusion", "Whoever consults will never regret it", "Seek help in your affairs through consultation."

Annadi (1999) argued that Islamic jurisprudence (Fiqh) presents Ash Shura as one of the most important concepts in jurisprudence and law and it dominates the thought of all Muslim scholars. Those scholars unanimously agree that Ash-Shura, as an obligatory act, obliges any Muslim ruler to consult and ask the opinion of those who are well versed in a given matter. The legitimacy of any Muslim ruler is determined by the extent of his adherence to this Kurān-based principle. It was not only Prophet Muhammad (Pbuh), but his companions and other Muslim Caliphs who ruled the Muslim nation after the Prophet, who observed and acted within this principle. Even the non-believers of the Prophet's time admitted that Ash-Shura as a principle was the result of a unique discernment aimed at the establishment of a righteous and stable society.

The Saudi general public and Muslims in general believe that this principle facilitates and induces all means of modification, development and progress. To realise such end-results, however, Al Awaji (1971) argued that the talent, capabilities and other assets to be invested in Majlis Ash-Shura should be carefully chosen so that proper and reliable advice can be practical and useful for the progress and development of society.

After the departure of the Prophet (Pbuh), adherence to the principles of Ash-Shura and its application continued during the reign of the righteous Caliphs creating several precedents. Abu Bakr, the first Caliph following in succession the Prophet Muhammad, when encountering a problem usually referred to the Kurān seeking a decision on a problem or matter. If he did not find guidance in the Kurān, he sought it in Al Sunna and if he did not reach a verdict on the issue, he resorted to the people, asking them: "Have you ever been informed that the Prophet had decided on that matter?" If one of them told him about such a decision, he would follow it. If not, he gathered the people and asked them to advise him and proceeded when they were unanimous.

Omar, the second Caliph, followed the same procedure. If he could not find a judgement in Islamic sources (Kurān and Sunna), he would consult people and follow the decision they reached. Al-Qassimi (1990) argued that Caliph Omar made the first steps towards organising Ash-Shura in the government system and he deemed it general on one part and special on the other. Caliph Omar said that

Muslims in general are obliged to consult those with expertise and specialisation and to consult with each other. He recognised that what had been said in the Kurān about Ash-Shura was the directive from which no single Muslim ruler should deviate. Caliph Omar went further by saying that the Muslim Caliph who is entrusted with ruling Muslims has no right to do so according to his own way of thinking. Instead, he should listen to the thoughts and ideas of experts and specialists. This, in terms of current affairs, means that the ruler or president must have beside him a council that makes, through majority, or consensus, decisions to be implemented by him.

5-2 Political Participation in Saudi Arabia

The Saudi strategy of introducing greater political participation has been echoed or anticipated in other Gulf states. The experiment in Oman is interesting. According to Peterson (1978) the Sultan's regime was subject to intense military and ideological pressure during the Dhufar rebellion of the early 1970s. With the defeat of the rebellion, overt political opposition all but
disappeared. A political public ethos was fostered by the government built upon a commitment to economic and infrastructural development under the leadership of Sultan Qaboos Ibn Said. Eickelman (1984) observed that a government-sponsored Majlis Ash-Shura was appointed in 1981. It was dominated by government members, met frequently, and had few powers. Eickelman also argued that by the time of the Gulf crisis, the political atmosphere in Oman was the most tranquil in the entire region. It thus came as a surprise to outsiders when the Sultan announced in November 1990 that Oman would have a new Majlis Ash-Shura with expanded powers and filled through indirect election on a provincial basis.

According to *Al-Hayat* (October 14, 1991), from May-June 1991 the provincial governors canvassed the notables in their areas to recommend three potential Majlis Ash-Shura members to the Sultan who then chose the members for that province. In some of the urban provinces, ballots were cast among attendees to determine the three nominees. Peterson (1978) argued that former government officials make up the largest group in Majlis Ash-Shura, with tribal leaders and businessmen also heavily represented. This system of indirect nomination by province is not a direct election from the perspective of democratic theory. The designation of notables is in the hands of the government, called into question the representative nature of the electorate. The provinces do not have equal population, so urban areas are under-represented in Majlis Ash-Shura. But the willingness to

78

bring some of the public into the process of nominating its representatives was an important departure from traditional Omani politics. In his opening address to Majlis Ash-Shura in December 1991, the Sultan asserted that Majlis Ash-Shura was a complete and equal branch of government, not part of, nor subject to the executive branch (*Al Hayat*, December 22, 1992, 4). Whereas members of the bureaucracy dominated the state Majlis Ash-Shura, government officials are not permitted to sit on the new Majlis Ash-Shura.

Eickelman (1989) says that the new Majlis Ash-Shura has greater legislative powers than its predecessor. It has the right to review all legislation regarding cultural, educational, social and economic issues and state development plans and to recommend amendments by a two-thirds vote. It also has the right to question those who head those ministries that deliver public services, such as Health, Education, Housing, Information, Electricity and Water. They must submit an annual report to Majlis Ash-Shura. The new Majlis Ash-Shura ended its first year of operation in October 1992 and displayed a spirit of independence from the government. Its most notable activity was its questioning of ministers. It was a new experience for the ministers, especially those who had spent two decades in government without ever having to answer in a public forum for their activities. The Sultan agreed to a decree that allows the election of Majlis Ash-Shura members directly by the people (*Al-Sharq Al-Awsat*, May 8, 2000).

An appointed Majlis Ash-Shura has also been established in Bahrain. In his National Day address of December 16, 1992, Sheikh Isa, Amir of Bahrain, announced his intention to establish such a body. By the beginning of 1993, 30 members were appointed. In this regard *Al-Hayat* (December 21, 1992) wrote that 18 of the members were merchants and/or contractors. Lawyers, religious judges, and doctors were also represented, as well as a journalist and a university professor. The Bahraini Majlis Ash-Shura held its first session in 1993. Lawson (1980) states that its powers are limited to the review of legislation sent to it by the Council of Ministers and to the oversight of government activity through the questioning of ministers. Unlike the Saudi experiment and the current Omani one, the changes in Bahrain do not have the same character of being a step forward. Lawson also observed that the original National Assembly in Bahrain, suspended in 1975, was directly elected and had extensive legislative powers. However, worries about the strength of Islamic political currents in religious communities in the country led the state to take the appointment route favoured in Saudi Arabia and Oman, rather than risk elections based on the Kuwaiti model.

In Qatar, Majlis Ash-Shura appointed in 1972 still sits. Its term is periodically extended so as to avoid the stipulation in the provisional constitution for elections.

In March 1993 the UAE Federal National Majlis Ash-Shura resumed meetings after a two-year gap. *Al Hayat* (March 2,1993) reported that seventy percent of its members, appointed by the rulers of the seven emirates, were new. The rumours that they would be chosen by direct election and that the powers of that body to initiate legislation and overturn government ministries would be expanded proved to be groundless.

The experience of the Gulf states in areas of political participation and representation is new and different in many of its aspects. There are no inherent cultural or historical impediments inhibiting the populace from participation in governmental affairs. Their respective governments allow them to advance their interests and participate effectively. The people can also form organisations referred to in the West as traditional tribal ties and Islamic institutions. Those traditional institutions have shown remarkable flexibility in adjusting to the circumstances of large bureaucratic states, modern technologies and dramatically changed economies. The growing role of the state in the life of citizens over the past twenty years has called forth new demands for political participation and government accountability, which these states have recently witnessed. As the state has come to mean more in peoples' everyday existence, they naturally want to have some control over the actions of the state. The vast expansion of educational opportunities, funded by the states' oil wealth, has enabled many more people to articulate their concerns in abstract and theoretical terms, rather than simply as personal appeals for individual favours.

Islam historically exhorted Muslim leaders in general and Saudi rulers in particular to adhere to the principles of Islam and practice consultation. The constitution of Islam can lead societies to prosperity and peace of mind in this life and thereafter. The principle of consultation has become a social as well as a political need. It has to be implemented and observed in any Muslim society that seeks progress in its quest for development. Fundamental to the principle of Islam, which is deeply rooted in the government tradition in the Saudi realm, this chapter asserts that the *Ash-Shura* process of consultation has been a religious practice exercised by the Prophet Muhammad (Pbuh) and successive *Caliphs*. This approach has been explained within a historic framework to show that rulers are

traditionally accustomed to observe *Ash-Shura* as demanded by the religion of Islam. In the course of the discussion in this chapter, it has been emphasised that an adherence to the principle of *Ash-Shura*, as exhorted by the religion of God, enhances the religious legitimacy of any Muslim government. An absence of this principle would undermine the legitimacy of the government. As a social and political phenomena, *Ash-Shura* has not emerged as a result of the social conditions endured by modern Saudi society, but rather emerged and has been practised, in essence, as a religious duty. Those who can be selected to serve on Majlis Ash-Shura should be:
1.   A Saudi national by birth.
2.   Known as having a good reputation and being well qualified.
3.   Not less than 30 years old.
4.   Pious, righteous, educated and with relevant experience.

The by-laws of Majlis Ash-Shura can be summed up as follows:

Firstly, a member of Majlis Ash-Shura has the right to resign to the speaker, and in turn the speaker should submit the matter to the King. If a member neglects his duties, an investigation should be conducted against him and he should be tried. If for any reason, a seat of a member falls vacant, the King will name an alternative by Royal decree. A member should not exploit his membership to serve his own interest. Members of Majlis Ash-Shura should not associate themselves with another private or public appointment unless the King should see a need for this. The speaker of Majlis Ash-Shura can and should appoint his deputy and the Secretary General of Majlis Ash-Shura. Their tenure in office, their salaries, rights and a Royal Decree determines duties and various other affairs related to their office.

In Royal Decree No. A/91, dated 1992 (the original Arabic version of these explanations) it is stated that the speaker, the members and the Secretary General of Majlis should take the following oath before taking up their appointments:

> I swear by Almighty Allah (God) that I shall remain faithful
> to my religion, to my King and country and never divulge a
> secret of State. I swear to preserve the interests of the State
> and its regulations and to perform my duties with truth,
> honesty, justice and faith.

81

The term of Majlis Ash-Shura is set for four years, with a clear stipulation that when a new Majlis Ash-Shura is formed, at least half of those appointed must be new members. The setting of fixed terms in this regard may indicate a shift away from the past policy of indefinite tenure of political office. The headquarters for Majlis Ash-Shura are to be based in Riyadh, but it may hold meetings elsewhere in the Kingdom if they are approved by the King. In terms of establishing a quorum, it was decreed that a Majlis Ash-Shura meeting requires the presence of two-thirds of its membership. For a Majlis Ash-Shura resolution to be legal, a simple majority vote is required. Majlis Ash-Shura resolutions are to be submitted to the Prime Minister who will refer them to the Council of Ministers. If the views of Majlis Ash-Shura and the Council of Ministers are in agreement, a royal approval will be issued. If the views of the two councils diverge, the matter will be referred to the King for a decision.

Majlis Ash-Shura has the right to express its opinions on the general policies of the state which are referred to it by the Prime Minister. Table 5.1 shows the exclusive functions of Majlis Ash-Shura.

Table 5.1   The Exclusive Functions of Majlis Ash-Shura

To discuss and express its opinion on the general policy for social and economic development.
To study and suggest what is proper and pertinent to the Kingdom's rules, regulations, tactics, international accords and concessions.
To interpret regulations.
To discuss and offer suggestions relating to the annual reports submitted by the ministers and others government departments.

Majlis Ash-Shura will be given the opportunity to review regulations, conventions, international agreements and principles before they are issued or duly amended by a Royal decree. Majlis Ash-Shura may also establish specialised committees made up of its members, to discuss items on its agenda. With the approval of the speaker, these committees may seek the assistance of non-members whose speciality qualifies them to provide advice.

5-3 Applications of Ash Shura in the Saudi Political System

The first Saudi Majlis Ash-Shura (Consultative Council) started when Imam Mohammad Ibn Su'ud and Sheikh Mohammad Ibn Abd – al wahhab used to consult men of knowledge during the time of war. The two men would call a temporary advisory council to assist the Imam.

During the reign of King Abd - al Aziz (1932 – 1953), every important state plan and decision was concluded based on opinions solicited from well-versed and righteous individuals. This approach was conducted through consultative methods. After the conquest of Makkah in 1924, King Abd - al Aziz held a meeting to consult experts and men of knowledge on how to outline a rule of law that could serve as the foundation for a permanent consultative assembly. According to Al Duraib (1984), The King made a statement in which he said that the goal of the state was to purify the holy land from all forms of bad practices and to apply the laws of Islam. He also said that "the King called for a Muslim conference to be attended by delegates from Muslim countries all over the world. The purpose of which was to decide on the form of Muslim government to execute the orders of God in the Holy Land. Ten days later, the King met with scholars from Makkah and asked them to hold a general convention with the participation of scholars, merchants and local notables in societal affairs and decision-making.

The purpose of such a gathering was to elect a number of individuals to act as representatives of the people. Khairidin Zarkally (1985, .69) argued that the convention was held within two days and a Majlis Ash-Shura was elected to represent and serve the public interest. That council was called the "Majlis Ash-Shura Al Ahli" (Domestic Consultative Council). It was comprised of twelve members and assumed its duties for six months. Later the King decided to expand the range of participation and accordingly he allowed free elections. The chairman of Majlis Ash-Shura and his deputy were elected by means of confidential voting. Al Duraib also stated that the duties and functions of the selected Majlis Ash-Shura would include overseeing municipal affairs, ensuring that equality and justice are observed by all local courts and ensuring that all state revenues are audited and allocated according to the laws of Islam. Majlis Ash-Shura was also given the duty of overseeing the police and security system in the region. It was expected that Majlis Ash-Shura would promote the means and methods of religious education. At this stage of progress, the King decreed that Majlis Ash-Shura could form committees to consider and settle local problems by means of consultation and without any violation of the laws of Islam.

Al Johany (1992) stated that after the outbreak of the Second World War, the King appointed his son Prince Faisal as deputy in the Hejaz area and assigned to him a consultative council of three members. An eight-member council was elected by Hejaz representatives (notables) along with an additional five members appointed by the King. A royal decree to this effect was issued pertinent to the cities of Medinah, Jeddah, Yanbu and Taif. All such councils were formed through elections. The scholars, merchants, notables, professionals and heads of vocations had the right to vote and elect. Elected members were to serve on Majlis Ash-Shura for one year only. According to Dahlan (1990), the King dissolved Majlis Ash-Shura, only to revive its activities and increase the members' term on the council to two years. The government through consultative means conducted by men of learning, selected half of the members of Majlis Ash-Shura. The government directly appointed the other. The new procedures enabled the elected Majlis Ash-Shura to carry out a number of activities, which included the budget of the government, overseeing government projects, enacting regulations and laws pertinent to expatriates and verifying contracts and auctions conducted and administered by government officials.

Al Johany (1992) maintains that this mechanism of Majlis Ash-Shura selection and its functions drew satisfaction from local communities simply because the essence of their practice was Islamic. Majlis Ash-Shura held 119 sessions, and adopted 221 resolutions during 1949. The three main committees in the assembly were: Finance, Rules and Regulations and Administrative Affairs. Within the first two years, Majlis Ash-Shura, with its affiliated committees, was very active. Fifty rules and regulations were issued. By-laws were issued along with regulations pertinent to such issues as education, the professions, business and customs. Majlis Ash-Shura continued its duties until 1953. During that term, 4,010 sessions were held and 7,239 resolutions were adopted.

With the formation of the Council of Ministers in 1953, some duties of Majlis Ash-Shura were re-assigned to the newly formed Council. However, Majlis Ash-Shura continued to convene on a regular basis and discuss all issues referred to it. In 1975 the number of members was increased to eleven and 754 sessions were held, with a total of 99 resolutions adopted. Here it can be noted that the number of sessions and the number of resolutions adopted decreased. The cause of this decrease was the transfer of some duties from Majlis Ash-Shura to the Council of Ministers.

5-4 Modern Formation of *Majlis Ash Shura*

Development of the state and the modernised mechanism of administration have necessitated the establishment of a Supreme Committee. That committee was entrusted to design strict regulations based upon which any future Majlis Ash-Shura could be founded. In 1982, King Fahad, then Crown Prince, chaired the sessions of the Supreme Committee. On March 1, 1992, having become King, he issued three royal decrees that established three important changes in the Saudi political system: (a) "The Basic System of Government" a constitution-like document (b) the Statute for a new Majlis Ash-Shura (Consultative Council) and (c) a System of Regional Government for the Kingdom's Fourteen Provinces. In his speech to the Saudi nation, King Fahad stated that there had been no vacuum in the Saudi political development cycle. The Saudi constitution is itself the Shari'a of Islam, for it is founded on the principles of the Kurān and the traditions of Prophet Muhammad (Pbuh). These two sources, as viewed by the Saudi officials and public alike, provide a reliable means of guidance once it has been adopted by any Muslim society. It is the general belief that through Ash-Shura no social or political formula is implemented unless it is in complete accord with the core of the religion of Islam. All regulations have to be in complete harmony with the text and spirit of the Kurān and above all should serve the interest of the people.

The essence of Shari'a is derived from the belief that the relationship between the governor and the governed should be based on mutual respect, a strong belief in the principle of brotherhood and an exchange of advice, goodwill and co-operation. The way the affairs of Muslims should be administered is deeply rooted in the Saudi traditions of love, compassion, justice and fair treatment for all. This approach is supported by the Kurānic verse which says:

> "And those who respond to God and perform prayers and hold consultations among themselves and spend of what we have made available to them." (*The Holy Kurān, Ash-Shura,* Verse 38.)

Article 68 of the Basic Law mandates the establishment of a Majlis Ash-Shura. By Royal decree, the King issued the founding statute of Majlis Ash-Shura that sets the membership of Majlis Ash-Shura at 60 members, along with a President, all appointed by the King (Article 3). Majlis Ash-Shura will have four-year terms and at least one-half of the membership of every Majlis Ash-Shura must be composed of new members (Article 13). Article 9 mandates that no member of the government is allowed to be a member in Majlis Ash-Shura and from the composition of the first Majlis Ash-Shura it is clear that ruling family members will not be appointed. Article 15 states that Majlis Ash-Shura has a wide mandate to comment on affairs of state, including "the general plan for economic and social development" and "administrative statutes and regulations, treaties and international agreements and concessions". Article 18 seems to imply that administrative regulation and treaties must be submitted to Majlis Ash-Shura for review. Ministers and state departments are required to submit annual reports to Majlis Ash-Shura for review and the president of Majlis Ash-Shura may request attendance of any government official at Majlis Ash-Shura sessions related to his responsibilities (Articles 15 and 22). The King or his representative will address Majlis Ash-Shura annually, "setting out the domestic and foreign policy of the Kingdom" (Article 14). Article 23 mandates that any ten members of Majlis Ash-Shura together have the right "to recommend a new administrative regulation, or an amendment to a new administrative regulation" to the president of Majlis Ash-Shura, who is then obliged to submit the recommendation to the King.

King Fahad appointed the 60 members of the first Majlis Ash-Shura in his Royal decree of August 20, 1993. The King chose its President, the former Minister of Justice Sheikh Mohammed Ibn Jubayr, in September 1992. The members seem to represent a cross section of the Saudi elite, including important constituencies like the religious establishment, technocrats, intellectuals, journalists, university professors, and merchants. Approximately one third of members are university professors. As far as the regional background of the members is concerned, at least ten Hejazis were appointed, "at least four Asiris, and at least two from the Eastern Province" (*Al Sharq Al Awsat*, August 22, 1993, .3).

Based on the above analyses it can be argued that Majlis Ash-Shura is not an elected body but rather a selected one. It is not a legislative body either, having no powers other than those of recommendation. The Council of Ministers remains the legislative body in the Kingdom. In Islam the ruler has absolute power as long as he observes the teachings of Kurān. He is responsible only to God and not to parliaments as in the secular political systems. Consultation is a must for the ruler but in the end he takes the decision which he thinks is right according to the teachings of Kurān and Sunna.

Figure 5.1 shows the administrative organisation of Majlis Ash-Shura as issued by its Chairman in 1994, thus defining the organisation. As can be observed, the Steering Committee, the Specialised Committees, the Chairman's Office, and the Advisors and Finance Departments report to the Chairman where all other departments are overseen by the Deputy Chairman. Eight committees, originally not represented in this chart, work under the Specialised Committees department and report directly to the Chairman. Each committee has a chairman and a co-chairman and up to 11 members. Committees are not represented in the organisational chart because they are to a certain extent self-contained and work parallel to Majlis Ash-Shura. These committees are listed in Table 5.2.

Table 5.2   Committees of Majlis Ash-Shura

Religious Committee
External Affairs
Security Affairs
Economic and Financial
Social and Health
Educational, Travel and Media
Services and Public Institutes
Political and Administration

Figure: 5:1

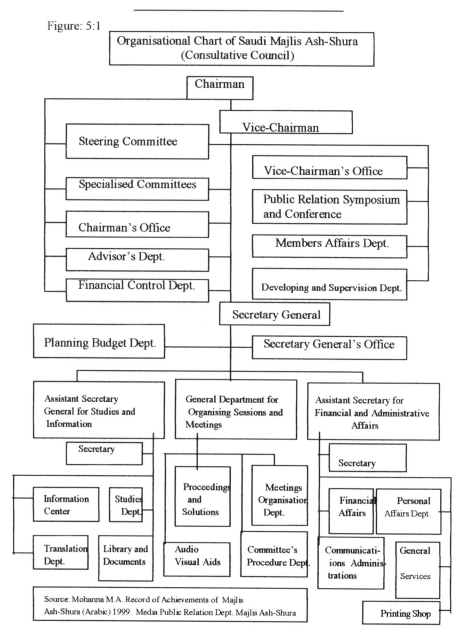

Organisational Chart of Saudi Majlis Ash-Shura
(Consultative Council)

Source: Mohanna M.A. Record of Achievements of Majlis
Ash-Shura (Arabic) 1999. Media Public Relation Dept. Majlis Ash-Shura

According to the by-laws of Majlis Ash-Shura, each committee should include no fewer than five members named by Majlis Ash-Shura. These committees can be modified as necessary. The chairman or his deputy, if he is not available, chairs its sessions. Majlis Ash-Shura committees meet by a call to order from its chairman, Majlis Ash-Shura, or Majlis Ash-Shura chairman. Its sessions are not public and its decisions are taken by majority vote. (Appendix II).

To provide further information on the official reaction and understanding of the Royal decrees, it can be added that in his speech the King pointed to the unique role of the Kingdom in the Muslim world. This belief is based on the history of Al - Su'ud's connection with the earlier Saudi reform movement and the family's custodianship of the holy sites of Makkah and Medina. To him, Western democracy is an inappropriate basis for politics in the peninsula. In an interview (*New York Times*, 30 March 1992, p.A6) the King said, "The nature of our people is different ... The democratic system prevailing in the world does not suit us in this region of the world."

Majlis Ash-Shura enjoys a strong sense of stability and complete freedom of self-expression. In this regard, Dhohayan (1992) argued that the voting procedures of Majlis Ash-Shura are characterised as free from any form of supervision. The issues debated by the assembly proved to be very effective for they influence the welfare of the people and the general economic and social development of the country. Majlis Ash-Shura has become a prominent political institution, with members from varied social and educational backgrounds. They can participate directly in law-enactment and consequently provide relevant advice to the ruler.

Chapter Six:

Survey of *Majlis Ash Shura*

6-1 Survey Techniques

A questionnaire (Appendix I) was designed as a tool for this research . The following is description of the steps that were followed in its preparation:

1. Before designing the study questionnaire, the author personally visited the Chairman of Majlis Ash-Shura, Sheikh Mohammed Bin Jubair. He also separately met three members. The reason for these meetings were to explain the study and discuss aspects related to the laws, policies and procedures of the Majlis. I also attended several real sessions of the Majlis to obtain first-hand knowledge about the manner and the method utilised in the discussions, voting and resolutions of Majlis Ahs-Shura.

2. The questionnaire was prepared considering the previously mentioned meeting and other variables that cover various aspects related to the study subject. It included sections on the demographic characteristics of members, for example, social and educational backgrounds, the operation of Majlis Ash-Shura and the opinions of the members on its various activities and their satisfaction with it. Finally, the questionnaire contained open-ended questions on member opinions related to strengths and weaknesses of the Majlis Ash-Shura and their suggestions on how to improve the efficiency and operations of the Majlis.

3. After preparing the first and reviewed draft of the questionnaire, a copy was handed to each of the following people:

    3.1   Sheikh Mohammed Bin Jubair, Chairman, Majlis Ash-Shura
    3.2   Dr. Homoud Al-Badr, Secretary General, Majlis Ash-Shura
    3.3   Dr. Fahd A. Al-Harthi, Member, Majlis Ash-Shura
    3.4   Dr. Bader Al-Ammaj, Member, Majlis Ash-Shura
    3.5   Dr. Mohammed Al-Helwa, Faculty of Political Science, King Su'ud University.

Input from meetings with the above panel and their comments were incorporated into the questionnaire to ensure its validity.

4. A pilot study on 4 members of Majlis Ash-Shura was conducted to test the questionnaire for practicality. It was modified on the recommendations of

these members and a final draft was obtained and distributed to all members of Majlis Ash-Shura through the Administrative Office of the Majlis as mentioned previously.

Reliability testing was conducted on the questionnaire using the Statistical Package for Social Sciences (SPSS) for Windows, Version 6. Two reliability tests were conducted separately on questions that have three possible answers and questions with five possible answers. The reason was to ensure that these questions are phrased properly to yield a consistent measurement result across of the survey.

Jaeger (1983) stated, "Reliability is a measurement concept that represents the consistency with which an instrument measures a given performance of behaviour". The split-half method is used in this survey to calculate the reliability coefficient of the study questionnaire. This procedure consists of splitting the total number of survey questionnaire items (odd and even) from a single administration of a single form of an instrument and correlating the two halves (Gall, 1989). Reliability coefficients have a value from zero to 1.0 the higher the coefficient is, the greater the reliability of the questionnaire (Borg and Gall, 1989).

To the following questions, it was possible to give one of three answers: 16A, 24, 25, 27, 33, 37, 46, 48, 49. The alpha Cronbach value of the reliability test was 0.77, which can be considered a good level. Therefore this part of the questionnaire may be considered to have high reliability.

The same test was repeated on questions with five possible answers: 12, 13, 14, 29, 35, 52. The alpha Cronbach value of the reliability test for these questions was 0.61 which could also be considered to have good reliability. Hence this part of the questionnaire can also be considered as having fairly high reliability. The justification for choosing the variables of the study are discussed in order of their appearance in the results report.

6-2 Results Analysis:

Table 6.1 shows the age distribution in the study sample. Of 38 members (42.2%) who responded by completing and returning the questionnaire, 28.6% of the sample were in the age group under 50 years (71.4% were in the age group 50 years or more). The age of members ranged between 41 and 71 years, with a mean age of 55.05 years and a standard deviation of 7.73. Standard deviation (SD)

91

shows the clustering of data around the mean. The higher standard deviation is, the more data is dispersed. This distribution reflects the presence of several generations of Saudi citizens.

Table 6.1 Age Distribution of Study Subjects

Age	Persons	Percentage
41-45	3	9
46-50	9	26
51-60	14	40
> 60	9	25
Total	35	100

Table 6.1 above shows that whilst 38 members (42%) responded to the questionnaire, three did not answer this specific question. 34% of the sample are in the age groups under 50 years; 71.4% were in the age group 50 years or above. The members' ages ranged between 41 to 70 years with a mean age of 55 years and S.D. 7.73. This age distribution is indicative of the fact that both old and young Saudi generations are represented in the assembly.

The following table shows the subject's place of birth.

Table 6.2   Place of Birth Distribution

Place of Birth	Persons	Percentage
Village	11	29
City	27	71
Total	38	100

A study of place of birth and growth would give a clue to their geographic affiliation and the areas represented by them in Majlis Ash-Shura. As it is shown in Table 6.2 none of the members were born in the desert. Eleven members (29%) were born in a village and 27 other members (72%) were born in cities.

92

Table 6.3 below shows the distribution of the study sample according to regional locations.

Table 6.3 Distribution of Study Sample According to Geographical Location

Area	Persons	Percentage
Central	14	37
Northern	3	8
Southern	2	5
Western	16	42
Eastern	3	8
Total	38	100

In comparison to other regions, the central and western regions are known to represent the highest population concentrations in the Kingdom. The table above shows that the central region is represented by 37% while the western region is represented by 42%. Again, this approach has come to prove that the density of population is proportionally represented in Majlis Ash-Shura.

Table 6.4 shows the percentage distribution of this educational variable.

Table 6.4 Educational Levels of Study Subjects

Education Degree	Persons	Percentage
BA	9	24
MA	5	13
Ph.D	24	63
Total	38	100

Table 6.4 shows that 75% of Majlis Ash-Shura members have reached the level of MA and/or Ph.D. from western universities. This is indicative that their learning and education had been obtained from reputable educational institutions. This is also indicative that the Saudi government has exerted considerable efforts to educate its citizens. This fact can be justified on the ground that 72% of the sample are still in their fifties, which means that the members of this age group

have availed themselves of the generous financial subsidies that the government had assigned to education. This distribution of the levels of education highlights the importance given to the academics to function and represent the interests of the public in Majlis Ash-Shura.

Pertinent to the education that the members have been exposed to, table 6.5 shows what percentage of them studied in a western or an Arab country.

Table 6.5 Distributions of Subjects According to Place of Study

Country	Person	%
Local Saudi University	5	14
Arab Country	3	8
Western Country	27	75
Other	1	3
Total	36	100

Here it can also be argued that the percentage obtained reflects the kind of Western or Arabic training that might have influenced the mentality of certain groups or members. In other words, their type of background training is viewed here as an additional personal trait.

Due to the importance of previous training and experience in regard to the achievement of any individual, a question to this effect was included in the questionnaire and the results are displayed in Table 6.6.

Table 6.6 Public Sector Experience

Range of Experience	Persons	Percentage
2 to 5 years	3	8
13 to 24 years	10	27
24 and above	24	65
Total	37	100

94

The majority of the sample studied proved to be experienced and well-trained in public sector services. About two thirds of the sample reported a work experience that exceeds 24 years. On the other hand, 47% of the members reported having had work experience in the private sector ranging from one to 21 years.

Table 6.7 illustrates specific information regarding the nature of the occupations exercised by the study subjects.

Table 6.7 Types of Previous Occupations

Type	No Experience	%	Experience	%
Administration	14	38	23	62
Business	33	89	4	11
Military	32	89	5	14
Academic	19	51	18	49
Other	27	73	10	27

Table 6.7 shows that 23 members (62%) have had administrative experience. Four (11%) practised business or commercial type of work, five (13%) were in the armed forces, and 18 (49%) were academics. This pattern can be explained by the high education level enjoyed by members. Given the statistical fact that more than half of the sample have had previous experience in an administrative sector, it can be argued that they have held leading government or public positions. Very few have had experience in business.

To explore an additional asset in the experience and personality of members on Majlis Ash-Shura, a study of the time that each member has had in the assembly was conducted with results shown in Table 8.

Table 6.8   Years of Service in Majlis Ash-Shura

Experience	Persons	%
<Two years	25	66
5 to 6 years	13	34
>six years	None	None

Based on the information included in the table above, 25 members (66%) were relatively new members, while 13 (34%) had spent between five and six years working in the assembly. The mean time period was 2.9 years, S.D. 2.0 and a range of 1-6 years. The relatively short length of service can be explained on the grounds that the modern form of Majlis Ash-Shura has only recently been developed.

Table 6.9 exhibits the belief and conviction of the sample members about reasons behind the initiation of the Saudi Majlis Ash-Shura. However, before commenting on the results displayed in this table, there is a need to discuss the reasons for the criteria adopted in this part of the research. It can be argued that a category of such criteria would give a clue to the belief that the members have when they decided to accept such a appointment. As a criterion relevant to this approach, "Expanding the range of responsibility" has been selected to establish if those members do believe that the range of responsibilities, as practised by high-ranking officials, has been parochial and should be expanded by additional constructive participation from the public. This approach is applicable to the second criterion, "A need to complete the building of government institutions". This criterion for selection was based on the inquisitive nature of the researcher. That is, the researcher wanted to know if the members believe that it is not the public participation in sharing responsibilities as much as a gap in the constitutional structure of the government that can be bridged by the establishment of such a Majlis Ash-Shura. This analysis is applicable to criterion number three.

Table 6.9   Reasons behind the Initiation of Majlis Ash-Shura

Reason	No	%	Yes	%
Expanding the range of responsibilities.	29	76	9	24
A need to complete the building of government institutions.	12	32	26	68
Encourage public participation.	12	32	26	68
Involve qualified Saudis in development.	11	29	27	71
Promote Ash-Shura work.	14	37	24	63
A need to develop present policies.	16	42	22	58

Criterion No. 4, "To involve qualified persons in development", is listed in the category in order to know whether the members really believe that, before the establishment of Majlis Ash-Shura the participation of qualified Saudis in the process of development had been limited and consequently the door has to be open to their participation through an official Council dictated by means of religion. If this is not what the members believe, then the establishment of Majlis Ash-Shura can be explained based on a need to develop present government policies as stated in criterion No. 6.

Based on the analysis above, it is arguable that the personal belief of the members is highly important because it can be an indirect indicative of the validity, performance and efficacy of Majlis Ash-Shura. An analysis of such criteria would explain, from the perspective of the most educated Saudis, the real need for this Council. In short, the criteria have been chosen based on a personal analytical perspective founded on a personal experience with the Saudi social, administrative and political spheres.

Based on the results stated in Table 6.9, it can be concluded that 24% of the members believe that the reason Majlis Ash-Shura was established has been to expand government responsibilities and allow a wide social stratum to participate in the government's functions and duties. The percentage of those who believe that the building of the state's institutions would be complete by Majlis Ash-Shura, amounts to 68%, or 26 the members surveyed. The percentage of those who oppose this approach amounted to 32%. The percentage of those who support the willingness of the government to expand the scope of public participation amounted to 68%. On the other side of this equation, there were 71% who support the belief that the government wanted to make use of the available qualified Saudi talent. Twenty-four members (63%) believed that the reason behind establishing Majlis Ash-Shura has been to emphasise Majlis Ash-Shura in a systematic way. The idea that there has been a need to upgrade and develop government policies and procedures was supported by 22 individuals (58%). The majority of the members on Majlis Ash-Shura reported a combination of the variables included in the category of adopted criteria. Seven members (18%) believe that there is a totality of the reasons that contribute to the establishment of Majlis Ash-Shura, while 31 members or (82%) are in favour of the last three reasons in the category of the criteria implemented.

A study of the reaction of the members to Majlis Ash-Shura would remain incomplete unless the opinions of the members regarding (1) the efficacy of the assembly in the process of decision making, and (2) the voicing of one's opinion (freedom of speech in the process of debate) are explored. This analytical approach is explained in Table 6.10, which is divided into three separate but relevant sections.

Table 6.10 (a)   The Efficacy of Majlis Ash-Shura

Range of Satisfaction	Persons	%
Very satisfied	11	29
Somewhat satisfied	24	63
Unsure	0	0
Somewhat dissatisfied	2	5
Very dissatisfied	1	3
Total	38	100

Table 6.10 (b) Decision Making

Range of satisfaction	Persons	%
Very satisfied	8	21
Somewhat satisfied	27	71
Unsure	1	3
Some what dissatisfied	2	5
Very dissatisfied	0	0
Total	38	100

Table 6.10 (c) Freedom to Voice an Opinion

Range of satisfaction	Persons	Percentage
Very satisfied	24	63
Somewhat satisfied	13	34

Unsure	0	0
Somewhat dissatisfied	1	3
Very dissatisfied	0	0
Total	38	100

Analysis of the figures listed in Table 6.10 (a) shows that 35 members (92%) were either somewhat satisfied or very satisfied with the issue of efficacy (a due fulfilment of duties and responsibilities). The percentage of those who are somewhat dissatisfied amounted to 5% while 3% reported to be very dissatisfied. Generally speaking, the total result pertinent to efficacy shows that the majority of the members are satisfied. Responses from those who are not satisfied can be viewed as individual responses and cannot be fitted into the adopted pattern. Besides, the 63% that reported as somewhat satisfied may mean that there is a strong potential for improvement in the efficacy of Majlis Ash-Shura.

Table 6.10 (b) shows that a majority (92%) of the 38 members were either somewhat satisfied or very satisfied with the freedom of speech observed in the process of deliberation. Just two members were somewhat dissatisfied.

Table 6.10 (c) shows that a majority of this sample were very satisfied with the process. This phenomenon could be an indication of a belief that the assembly members enjoy freedom to express their opinions. Such freedom makes room for the conduct of intellectually meaningful debates by educated assembly members.

At the level of technicalities, the time factor was researched because it was viewed as a supportive factor in the process of decision making. Table 6.11 shows the reaction of the sample members to the time granted to them to review an issue before passing a vote.

Table 6.11 Availability of Enough Time to Review Issues Before Voting

Availability of Enough Time	Members	Percentage
Yes	27	37
No	9	24
Most of the time	1	39
Total	37	100

99

The figures in Table 6.11 show that 27 members (73%) indicated that they are allowed enough time to review or collectively discuss an issue before an official session is held. Nine members (24%) stated that they are not allowed such time. Only 1 member (3%) claimed that in most cases members are allowed enough time to deliberate and exchange opinions before formal sessions are held. This sort of discrepancy means that the members are not entirely satisfied with this technicality. It also means that the question of a time factor can affect, in one way or another, a unanimous decision by the members. Some claim that they usually have enough time to review a case while others would say that they are rushed in official sessions, where they have to voice their opinions spontaneously. Members were asked to provide an example but they declined to do so. The question of pressure that the government might exercise on members of Majlis Ash-Shura was researched as a phenomenon rejected by both western and traditional Islamic standards. Being a highly important issue with consequences that can have negative effects on the very essence of Majlis Ash-Shura, Table 6.12 shows the responses of the sample study.

Table 6.12 Government Pressure Distribution

	Persons	%
Yes	0	0
No	34	90
Rare	4	11
Total	38	100

The figures listed in Table 6.12 show that the majority of the 34 sample members (90%) stated that they have not been exposed to any form of pressure from the government. Four members (11%) argued that some pressure from the government had been exercised, although examples of such pressure were not provided in the response to the questionnaire.

The issue of the efficacy of the decisions concluded by Majlis Ash-Shura is discussed in order to answer the question: "Are those decisions ratified, valued and adopted by the government?" Again this phenomena was researched to show the validity of the decisions adopted by Majlis Ash-Shura and subsequently the effect of this Islamic political and social phenomenon in the process of national development. Result of the interaction between decisions adopted and the effectiveness of Majlis Ash-Shura are shown in Table 6.13.

Table 6.13   **Response of Council of Ministers to Majlis Ash-Shura Resolutions**

Reaction	Persons	%
Reacts negatively	0	0
Reacts positively	34	89
Rarely reacts	3	8
No answer	1	3
Total	38	100

Table 6.13 shows that 34 members (89%) claimed that the government, upon taking important or strategic decisions, adopts decisions concluded by the assembly. Eight of the group of 34 (21%) claimed that this occurs all the time while the other 26 members (69%) mentioned that this adoption on the part of the government happened sometimes. Three members stated that the government rarely adopted decisions concluded by Majlis Ash-Shura, while one member opted not to answer.

The awareness of the general public about the efficacy of Majlis Ash-Shura as viewed from the prospective of its members was also researched. It is meant by this discussion to get an idea about the impact of the presence of the public in the minds of the members while handling nation related issues. The figures obtained have been as follows: One member (2%) believed that the general public was well acquainted with the efficacy of Majlis Ash-Shura; 7 members (18%) believed that awareness is somewhat high, 8 members (21%) abstained. The other aspect of the study showed that 11 members (29%) believed that this awareness is somewhat low, 10 members (26%) believed that public awareness was very low. More than half of the members believed that the public awareness of the efficacy of Majlis Ash-Shura was low. They attributed this low percentage of awareness to causes such as: an inadequate media coverage of Majlis Ash-Shura activity, lack of illustrative pamphlets and brochures and the secrecy or confidentiality of the sessions conducted by Majlis Ash-Shura. With regard to the question of representation, it seemed that 19 members (50%) believed that Majlis

Ash-Shura represents individual social groups, while a similar number of members believe that Majlis Ash-Shura represents, to a certain degree, the whole of society. But there was a general agreement that Saudi society is, more or less, represented in Majlis Ash-Shura. The more members of the assembly, the more the Saudi population is represented.

Concerning the issue of membership selection, a related study was conducted and the figures are shown in Table 14.

Table 6.14   Selection Criteria

Type	Yes Persons	%	No Persons	%
Region	20	53	18	47
Social /tribal	10	26	28	74
Education/general knowledge	36	95	2	5

Table 6.14 shows that the vast majority of the sample of 36 members, 95% believed that the criteria for selecting the members was founded on educational bases. Twenty members (53%) have attributed it to choices based on regional consideration e.g. geographical balance of representation. Ten members (26%) have attributed the criterion of selection to tribal and social considerations (tribal influence). Regardless, preference was, generally speaking, given to educational and experience qualifications, but still the door is left open to those known for their wisdom, social leverage, piety and righteousness. The fact that more than half of the members support the geography and region related criteria can be explained on the ground that the government is keen to have all regions in the Saudi realm represented in Majlis Ash-Shura. That explains the selective approach exercised by the government. The widespread but sparse distribution of the Saudi population in the desert justifies this approach. Even though Saudi society is traditionally tribal, it can be seen that only 26% of the members attribute the cause of selection to tribal and social status criteria. This is an indication to the social and moral process of thinking that has started to prevail and characterize the mentality of the Saudi general public, besides Saudi Arabia is a highly urban country.

Chapter Seven:
Assessment of *Majlis Ash Shura*

7-1 Members' Reactions to Majlis Ash-Shura Achievements

The achievements that exhibit the efficiency and dynamic nature of Majlis Ash-Shura include:

1.   The increase of 60 to 90 Majlis members during the second session. That increase has allowed the participation of as many citizens as possible in the decision making process and the provision of consultation. Further, this increase may indicate more participation and a greater breadth of activity within Majlis Ash-Shura.

2.   The increase of the number of committees from eight to eleven. As a result of this increase, some committees have been split into two committees each. An example of this is the committees of finance, economy, education and information.

3.   Giving opportunities to various dignitaries to attend parts of Majlis Ash-Shura sessions, as was the case during the second year when the Ministers of Finance, Foreign Affairs, Planning and Education attended sessions, to become acquainted with government policies and answer the inquires of the members. Later, HRH Prince Naif Bin Abd - al Aziz, the Minister of Interior, and in capacity as Chairman of Manpower in addition to the Minister of Labour and Social Affairs, visited Majlis Ash-Shura to discuss issues relevant to workers and working manpower and providing job opportunities to graduates from Saudi universities. At that time, a committee that has been founded for this purpose submitted decisions to higher authorities to find solutions to labour problems and to replace the foreign work force by a Saudi one.

4.   Majlis Ash-Shura Chairman recalls that Majlis Ash-Shura has already consulted women on specific issues, especially those specialised in social affairs. Majlis Ash-Shura, he adds, accepts participation from women, but they are not allowed yet to become members of Majlis Ash-Shura.

5.   Recently, Majlis Ash-Shura has held public sessions and discussed issues related to press regulations. The sessions were attended by chief editors from a number of major local newspapers.

To be acquainted with the opinions of Majlis Ash-Shura members on its efficiency in performing its missions and practising its actions and role in rationalising the political decisions, two questions were included in the questionnaire. The following findings have been arrived at:
1.   The Efficacy of Majlis Ash-Shura in Performing Majlis Ash-Shura missions:

To identify Majlis Ash-Shura efficiency in this regard, Majlis Ash-Shura members were asked how satisfied they were with the performance of the Majlis. Table 7.1 shows the response.

Table 7.1   Members Satisfaction with their Majlis Ash-Shura Performance Level

Satisfaction	Frequency	%
Very satisfied	11	29
Satisfied to some extent	24	63
Not satisfied to some extent	2	5
Not satisfied absolutely	1	3
Total	38	100

Table 7.1 shows that the majority of the members (63%) are to some extent satisfied with Majlis Ash-Shura performance. Next is the category of those who are very satisfied (29%), while 8% of Majlis Ash-Shura members were either not satisfied at all or satisfied only to some extent. This result shows a very high satisfaction level in that the satisfaction in Majlis Ash-Shura and its efficiency in performing its tasks. This may be attributed to the achievements of Majlis Ash-Shura during the last years, and the awareness of the members of the significance of these achievements and their role in promoting development in the Kingdom.

There are only three dissatisfied members. Their stance can be explained on the ground that they see the work volume and the achievements of Majlis Ash-Shura as below the level claimed. They might believe there is a need for further development at the performance level. Their views also are an indication of the democratic atmosphere prevalent in the Majlis where members freely indicate their dissatisfaction with the performance of the Majlis and opt for a higher level of achievement.

2.   Majlis Ash-Shura's role in rationalising the political process:

Table 7.2 shows the responses of members to the question relevant to the role played by Majlis Ash-Shura, and how it is viewed by the members, in the process of rationalising political decisions.

Table 7.2 The Role of Majlis Ash-Shura in Rationalising Political Decisions

Role of Majlis Ash-Shura	Frequency	%
Very useful	19	50%
Useful to some extent	18	47%
Not sure	1	3%
Not useful	-	-
Total	38	100%

These results indicate that half the respondents (50%) considered Majlis Ash-Shura very useful in rationalising the political decisions adopted by the government. The other half (47%) states that it was useful to some extent, while there was one member who was not sure about the usefulness of this approach. None of the members, however, identified this role as without use.

These findings show that almost all respondents were convinced that Majlis Ash-Shura's role is useful in rationalising government decision. This may be ascribed to the fact that Majlis Ash-Shura's includes experts, scholars and highly qualified citizens who are capable of providing the government with proper and useful opinions and recommendations that help it to reach proper or right decisions. This was obviously expressed by one of the members who wrote:

> "Majlis Ash-Shura's resolutions have great impact on the government's final decision-making process because these resolutions are made by various experts of different academic backgrounds."

Another member stated:

> "The influence is great because the collective decision helps the King to make a decision with confidence."

Seventeen members echoed these views by noting that Majlis Ash-Shura of Ministers follows, in most cases, Majlis Ash-Shura resolutions. Another member argued that:

> "The influence is positive and this can be seen from the congruency of decisions made by the government and Majlis Ash-Shura in most cases."

Three members quoted the subject of electricity-tax bills not approved by Majlis Ash-Shura as an example. In this regard one of the members stated:

> "The effects of decision-making began to appear. It is obvious that the government does not take any decision before consulting Majlis Ash-Shura. It always consults

106

Majlis Ash-Shura, specially on decisions relevant to the re-structuring of the electricity sector where Majlis Ash-Shura resolutions were obvious in the government's final decision."

One member described the influence applied by *Majlis Ash-Shura* on the government's decisions, saying:

"The impact or influence is potentially great, because Majlis exercises a retrospective monitoring role regarding the performance of the various ministries. The decision maker (King) transferred highly significant issues to Majlis even after the ministry concerned had decided on these issues."

On the other hand, one member sees that the influence of Majlis Ash-Shura and its deliberations on the government decisions is "limited". Another member sees the influence varies with the subject in question, while another member differentiates between Majlis Ash-Shura deliberations and its resolutions saying that:

"The influence of Majlis Ash-Shura deliberations is limited, but its resolutions have great influence on the final decision adopted by the King."

Generally speaking, most members agree that the resolutions of Majlis Ash-Shura influence the political decision-making process provided they are in harmony with the Ministerial decisions of Majlis Ash-Shura. If the resolutions are inconsistent, the final decision is the responsibility of the King.

This approach is in accordance with Article 17 of Majlis Ash-Shura system, which states:

Resolutions of Majlis Ash-Shura shall be submitted to the Prime Minister (The King) who shall refer them to the Council of Ministers for consideration. If views of the two Majlis Ash-Shuras are identical, a Royal Decree will

be issued; but if the views are not in agreement, then the king decides whatever he deems fit.

From the above discussions it follows that actions and achievements of Majlis Ash-Shura are not limited only to the study of regulations, treaties and opinions, but also issues resolutions and recommendations that have obvious influence on the government's final decisions, especially those concerned with the enactment of regulations (laws) or related amendments.

This highlights the importance of the role exercised by Majlis Ash-Shura in the political life in the Kingdom of Saudi Arabia. It also reflects the significance of its actions and contributions in modernising the regulations of the state and accelerating the wheel of development on a scientific basis, and helps the government to deal with the challenges of the present state of affairs.

7-2 Points of Strength of Majlis Ash-Shura

This study seeks to identify the major characteristics and strengths that characterised Majlis Ash-Shura from the members' point of view. The study questionnaire included the following question: "What are the major positives and points of strength that characterised Majlis Ash-Shura from your own point of view?" The responses were classified into twelve points of strength. The findings are shown in Table 7.3.

Table 7.3 The Positives and the Points of Strength that Characterise the Saudi *Majlis Ash-Shura*

No.	Points of Strength	Frequency
1.	High efficiency and effectiveness of performance	21
2.	It includes a unique combination of the society	19
3.	Freedom of opinion and articulation	15
4.	Openness and objectivity in discussions	14
5.	Absence of the various forms of coalitions and affiliations	10
6.	Gives precedence to the public interest	9
7.	The dominance of unique personal relationships	8
8.	Dependence on the Kurān and Prophet's Sunna	6
9.	Represents social status and sects	4
10	Takes its resolutions according to a majority vote	4

.		
11 .	Includes governmental organisations in the discussion	3
12 .	Other points of strength	5

The results in Table 7.3 show that there are positive aspects and points of strength that characterise Majlis Ash-Shura. Its high efficiency in performing its works was the leading aspect, followed by unique combination of citizens, the freedom of opinion and objectiveness during discussions, the absence of coalitions and ideological affiliations and the precedence of the public interest. In addition to unique human relationships within Majlis Ash-Shura, its dependence on the Holy Kurān and Sunna of the Prophet, its representation to society status and sects, the taking of resolutions on a majority basis and the inclusion of governmental organisations in the dialogues are all noted.

The points of strength stated in Table 7.3 will be discussed and analysed in the light of the details obtained from the members' responses. Also, the information and remarks that are made available for the researcher in this regard will be discussed.

7-3 Efficiency and Performance

The findings of the study make it clear that Majlis Ash-Shura is characterised by considerable efficiency, good judicial practice, a high level of achievement, and contributions to the service of the state and society.

The major indicators of the effectiveness of Majlis Ash-Shura and its efficiency in performing its works are the following:

1. Intensive meetings, including regularity of sessions in the specified time, which have never been postponed owing to the lack of a quorum.
2. The availability of specialised work committees to prepare topics efficiently and to make them ready for discussion.
3. A continuous high level of attendance in both Majlis Ash-Shura and the committee meetings.
4. An active contribution from the majority of members, in addition to enthusiasm and sincerity.
5. Majlis Ash-Shura has achieved various important works and made great contributions within the range of its authority and jurisdiction, mainly in the

109

study of the regulations, by-laws, treaties, and international agreements that have been referred to it by the King. In addition to studying the annual reports received from ministries and government departments, Majlis Ash-Shura has discussed aspects of the drawbacks and points of strength relevant to these systems and departments and recommended appropriate action to increase their efficiency and reduce expenses.

There are three other indicators that point to the growth of Majlis Ash-Shura workload and the size of responsibility cast on it. These indicators are:
1. The increasing of membership from 60 to 90 members. There have been calls for a further increase.
2. The increasing of the number of specialised committees from 8 to 11. Some members call for more.
3. Majlis Ash-Shura convened two sessions per week in addition to meetings held by specialised committees. The by-laws of Majlis Ash-Shura require the convening of one normal session at least each fortnight.

7-4 The Unique Incorporation of a Wide Social Range in Majlis Ash-Shura

One of the major characteristics of Majlis Ash-Shura is that it includes a unique combination of people. Members are selected on the basis of integrity, scientific specialisation and practical experience. With regard to points of strength one of the members argued, "Its inclusion of a selection of the best intellectuals, and educated people is a factor rarely included in any democratic system". Majlis Ash-Shura members are selected and appointed by the King. In this regard a special procedure is adopted where high-ranking officials in the government are nominated, based on considerations such as education, their area of speciality, previous experience and training, talent and righteousness. This is attributed to the fact that "membership has been done by selection and not by election" as stated by one member. He argued that this is a

part of Majlis Ash-Shura advantages and one of its basic characteristics. Many members pointed to the selection of Majlis Ash-Shura members as successful. The majority of the members have specialised scientific background and training, with wide administrative experience. This characteristic is not attainable for many similar parliaments whose members are elected, for in such circumstances unqualified members are likely to be elected. It also allows the possibility of the election of a corrupt member. This does not mean, however, that it is not possible

110

to develop a system for elections that may avoid these negative aspects and disadvantages.

7-5 Freedom of Opinion and Expression

One of the characteristics of Majlis Ash-Shura emphasised by its members is the freedom to express opinions during discussions and decision making concerning all topics and issues referred to Majlis Ash-Shura. In addition, it gives the chance for anyone to contribute with an ample time given to hearing all types of opinion. About this phenomenon, one member said, "There is the utmost freedom in Majlis Ash-Shura discussions and decision making". Another member said, "It is freedom that one feels in expressing one's views". A third member said, "There is a high level of freedom in the field of research and the field of speech". Another member emphasised that Majlis Ash-Shura is witnessing "an open discussion without any restriction or direction from someone else".

7-6 Openness and Objectivity in Discussions

The provision of the freedom of opinion and speech in Majlis Ash-Shura contributed to the emergence of more of its important characteristics. These are: openness, genuineness, and objectivity in the exchange of ideas and in discussion. One member pointed out, "There exists the utmost frankness between members during discussions". Another member pointed to the "objectivity and genuineness in exchanging ideas and discussion". Many members referred to "the openness in the interjections" in addition to the "objectivity and reality in handling subjects and expressing opinions freely". It is obvious that interjections occur without restriction or unseeming anger. The findings of the study assure that Majlis Ash-Shura sessions and meetings are distinguished by a civilised manner of presentation and constructive discussion between members. A considerable number of members pointed to "the civilised manner of presentation and discussion". This may be attributed to the brotherly human relations between members (see below).

7-6 The Absence of Coalitions and Affiliations

Majlis Ash-Shura is characterised by the absence of parties, groups, regional coalitions or affiliations between members. Some members admire the "absence of parties and stress the Saudi group spirit". This impartiality in purpose and fairness in references to particular situations and trends because of party or personal purposes are aspects that make voting incline toward the national interest, as one member stated. This idea was emphasised by another member who said:

"Each member owns his opinion in the voting process and he is not obliged or committed to another group".

7-7 The Public Interest

The logical consequence of the absence of partiality or groups and the absence of personal interests among Majlis Ash-Shura members is that they exhibit the public interests as a common target, held dear by all members. This public interest outweighs any personal or regional interest. This fact is assured by one member who says: "Unity of target: all are working to the interest of the country". Another member described what goes on in Majlis Ash-Shura as "real deliberation for what may serve the interest of the Country". Another member emphasised "the absence of personal interests of Majlis Ash-Shura members". Majlis Ash-Shura experience is benchmarked by the absence of private or party interest.

7-8 Human Relationships

One of the obvious points of strength in Majlis Ash-Shura is the existence of brotherly relations between its members. Co-operation, mutual respect and a collective spirit despite differences of opinions in some cases distinguish these relations. More than one member referred to this phenomenon saying: "brotherly and human relationships", "good relations between members", "mutual respect for the opinions of others and respect for opposing views", and the like. This is not only limited to relationships between members, but expands to include their relationship with the Chairman, his Deputy, and the Secretary General. There is no doubt that positive human environment and brotherly relationships between the members help to perform the work and duties with confidence and efficiency.

7-9 Dependency on the *Kurān* and the Prophet's *Sunna*

One of the major characteristics distinguishing Majlis Ash-Shura from all other parliaments and legislative assemblies in other countries is that it depends on the Holy Kurān and the Prophet's Sunna. Majlis Ash-Shura in all its works and practices is guided by the Kurān and the Sunna. Majlis Ash-Shura is committed not to violate the law of Islam stated in these two sources (the Kurān and Al Sunna). It is also considered to be the practical implementation of the principle of "Shura" that is brought by Islam and stated in the Kurān in more than one verse. This matter boosts its strength and legitimacy.

Majlis Ash-Shura regulations in this respect are emphasised in Article 1, which indicates that the Majlis performs its works in accordance with its regulations and the fundamental law exhorted by the Kurān and the Prophetic Sunna.

The findings of the study are in accord with this fact. One member stated;

"It represents the principle of consultation".

One member summarised this matter and elaborated its importance when asked about the major advantages and points of strength of Majlis. He said:

> "Being dependent on the Kurān and Al Sunna and the directive of God in itself is a unique process and a point of strength that should be consolidated and set as an example to be followed and enhanced. It is necessary to pursue development, and improvement, as a alternative approach to other global experiences."

7-10 The Representation of Society and Sects

The evidence of four members shows that Majlis Ash-Shura represents the status of Saudi society, its classes, its sects and the different regions of the country. One member said that Ash-Shura is distinguished because "it represents all social sects". Another one wrote: "It widely represents the various social strata and regions of the Kingdom". A third member pointed to "the geographical coverage the whole country."

It seems that the term 'representation of the social strata' means that academic categories and development sectors are represented mainly when an emphasis is given to factors such as the area of specialisation and previous experience. This explains why Majlis Ash-Shura incorporates members from various vocations and areas of speciality. Even though this is the basic approach, still there are members on Majlis Ash-Shura from various regions of the Kingdom. This phenomenon is attested to by the opinions expressed by Majlis Ash-Shura members when they were asked about the basic norms and regulations that should be considered for selecting Majlis Ash-Shura members. Ninety percent of the members gave the education and experience factors a priority. One member argued that in the process of selecting a Majlis Ash-Shura member, the development sectors in Saudi Society should be given a priority, e.g. Agriculture, Industry, Trade and Commerce, Business and similar.

113

7-11 Resolutions by Majority

The responses of four members pointed to a matter that characterises the Majlis: "decisions are taken on a majority basis", or as stated by another, "decisions are taken a simple majority". This makes the resolution of Majlis Ash-Shura and its recommendations reflective of the opinion and views of the majority.

7-12 Inclusion of Governmental Organisations in Discussions

One of the issues implemented in Majlis Ash-Shura and proved to be effective in enriching its work is that Majlis Ash-Shura is keen to include the relevant governmental organisations and departments in its discussions, starting from the initiation of committee works up to reaching to appropriate decisions. Representatives of these bodies can attend the sessions. Majlis Ash-Shura benefits from the experiences of qualified and specialised people who are not Majlis Ash-Shura members but who come from both government and the private sector. Majlis Ash-Shura also permits citizens regardless of gender to attend its sessions after co-ordination with the Department of Public Relations.

7-13 Other Points of Strength

Some members talked of other characteristics of Majlis Ash-Shura, such as the availability of various and different specialities that enrich discussions.

The results of this research study prove that Majlis Ash-Shura has become an effective political institution in the Saudi state. This belief can be verified and attested based on the volume of achievements and the important role played by Majlis Ash-Shura in orienting the Saudi political decision. It is this that makes the majority of Majlis Ash-Shura members pleased with the efficacy of Majlis Ash-Shura. It is expected that Majlis Ash-Shura will develop in both performance and its contribution to political drive, encouraging the realisation of increasing comprehensive development in Saudi society. This prospective approach is justified owing to the unique characteristics of Majlis Ash-Shura and other positive aspects that have been extracted as a result of this research study. Among its salient characteristics is that Majlis Ash-Shura has substantially been dependent on laws and regulations derived from the Shari'a. This approach, as such, is an implementation and an adherence to the consultation principle cited in the Kurān. Adherence to the consultation principle enhances the legitimacy of Majlis Ash-Shura. The results of the research study have exhibited the following points as among the strongest merits of Majlis Ash-Shura:

1.   Remarkable and effective history in the performance of tasks and duties.

2.   The quality of the members and their selection is based on specialisation and previous experience.
3.   Freedom of speech in the process of deliberation and decision-making.
4.   Frankness, seriousness and objectivity in all sessions.
5.   An absence of all forms of affiliations and groupings among members – a phenomenon that suggests that the interest of the general public is given the highest priority.

7-14 Difficulties and Points of Weakness

Majlis Ash-Shura has become a politically effective organisation that performs a tangible role in Saudi political life. We can argue that Majlis Ash-Shura has many positive, as well as unique points of strength and characteristics. However this does not imply that Majlis Ash-Shura is free of points of weaknesses. It does not mean either that its experience and work over the past years has not suffered from problems, errors or difficulties. Majlis Ash-Shura, is relatively speaking, a new organisation in regard to the form, structure and methods by which it performs its work. The establishment of this Majlis Ash-Shura is counted as a form of political modernisation that the Custodian of the Two Holy Mosques King Fahd is keen to introduce in the ruling system of the country. It is well known that any newly emerging establishment in society will face problems and impediments at the beginning of its work. Therefore it was expected that the Saudi Majlis Ash-Shura would face problems and difficulties, as well as create errors during the first years of its work. It is also expected that these problems and difficulties will continue until they are gradually eliminated due to the gradual maturing of its experience.

This study is in part an attempt to reveal the major drawbacks and points of weakness from the point of view of Majlis Ash-Shura members because they are the people best qualified to diagnose the real problems of Majlis Ash-Shura and the other difficulties that it faces. The study questionnaire includes two direct questions addressed to the members about the difficulties of Majlis Ash-Shura and the difficulties that faced them during their work in Majlis Ash-Shura.

While verifying and analysing the responses to these questions, the researcher has found that they are greatly interrelated and that it is very difficult to them. Some members separately identified separate the difficulties that face them with reference to the drawbacks and points of weakness of Majlis Ash-Shura. In contrast, other members expressed the points of weakness of Majlis Ash-Shura with reference to the difficulties and barriers that face them in their work. For this

115

reason, the answers to these two questions were dealt with during the analysis and discussion as one unit, or as two faces of the same coin. They are classified into ten categories in the manner shown in Table 7.4.

Table 7.4 The and Points of Weakness of _Majlis Ash-Shura_ as Stated by Members

No	Difficulties and Points of Weakness	Freque ncy
1.	Weakness of support and information system	29
2.	Restriction of the authorities and jurisdiction of Majlis Ash-Shura	24
3.	A shortage of managerial and financial capabilities	17
4.	Weakness of interaction with society and its desires	14
5.	The refusal of some members to participate in the work of Majlis	13
6.	The plurality of the relation between Majlis Ash-Shura and the government	12
7.	Difficulties in regard to the style of discussion and decision making	12
8.	Absence of the prior provision of an agenda and document in sufficient time before sessions	9
9.	Difficulties that relate to the regulations of Majlis	4
10.	Other difficulties	6
	Total	140

Table 7.4 shows the aspects of weakness of the Saudi Majlis Ash-Shura as perceived by its members. The difficulties and points of weakness are related to equipment, support services and information, which hold a leading position (21%). That is followed by the restrictions of the authorities and jurisdictions of Majlis Ash-Shura (17%). Shortage of managerial and financial capabilities ranked third (12%). A weakness of interaction with society and its desires ranked fourth (10%).

116

Three difficulties came in equal frequency namely, the decline of some members participation in the work of Majlis Ash-Shura, the plurality of relation between Majlis Ash-Shura and the government and the difficulties related to the style of discussion and decision making, with a frequency of 9% each. This was followed by the issue of lack of circulating the work schedule and documents in an ample time before sessions (6%). In the last place came the difficulties related to the regulations of Majlis Ash-Shura and its internal by-laws (3%). Other miscellaneous difficulties and points of weakness had a frequency of 4%.

It is obvious that weakness of support and a lack of a strong information system, the restriction of the authorities and jurisdictions of Majlis Ash-Shura and the shortage of managerial and financial capabilities, are major points of weakness of Majlis Ash-Shura. At the same time these factors are considered major difficulties that face the members. They hinder the process of their performance in Majlis Ash-Shura. The researcher himself had witnessed some of these difficulties and barriers during a visit to Majlis Ash-Shura. These barriers are emphasised by most of the members interviewed during the field visit to collect information for this study. These difficulties and aspects of weakness can be justified on the ground that Majlis Ash-Shura is still in its first years and that its experience is not yet mature and its managerial systems and support service are incomplete. It is believed that once these factors are taken care of, its authority will be expanded, its jurisdictions enforced, and the participation of members will be more effective. Some of the members referred to the importance of the time factor and the need to give members more time before a judgement or an evaluation is conducted. For example, one of the members said: "The drawbacks are few and there is time enough to overcome them". Another member stated: "We should wait until Majlis Ash-Shura is well developed; then we will be able to judge it because we are now involved in a new experience".

One member pointed out that difficulties facing the performance of the work of Majlis Ash-Shura are expected. It is natural that members will face administrative difficulties in dealing with some governmental organisations and ministries. He also argued that most of these difficulties can be eliminated after Majlis Ash-Shura has established practical rules to follow.

7-15 Weakness in both Support and Information Systems
A weakness in support and information systems tops the list of difficulties and barriers that confront the members of Majlis Ash-Shura (Table 7.4). Many members referred to this aspect in their answers to the questionnaire of this

research. One of them pointed out that one of the main difficulties confronting them is "lack of a sufficient support team for the member". Another member stated that the facilities available for members "are not sufficient". In short, members of Majlis Ash-Shura referred to the following points of weakness and difficulties:

Table 7.5 Points of Weakness and Difficulty

Weakness in the secretarial system.
Lack of genuine and valid information.
A limited role of the Department of Studies and Information.
Lack of information, documents and studies necessary to study issues that are put forward for discussion.
Lack of fundamental tools and factors to conduct studies and data collection.
Lack of researchers, assistants and translators.
Lack of necessary references, reading material and documents in the library
Low utilisation of information and communication technology: members do not have direct access to the internet and do not have an international telephone facility.
Deficiency of consultants in Majlis Ash-Shura and its committees.

It is obvious that these problems are a real hindrance to the task because the nature of the job of Majlis Ash-Shura demands the availability of supportive and qualitative services. There is also a need for data services characterised by accuracy and speed in performance. The nature of the job demands the conduct of scientific research that can support Majlis Ash-Shura's performance and its decision-making process. Thus these hindrances have to be eliminated.

Therefore, a recommended method towards realising that end, and a resort to the use of modern technology is highly recommended.

7-16 The Restriction of Authority and Jurisdiction of Majlis Ash-Shura

The outcomes of the study suggest that from the members' points of view the restriction of authority and jurisdiction is the second major barrier and point of weakness of Majlis Ash-Shura. The following are the main responses of the members in this regard:

Table 7.6 Restriction of Authority and Jurisdiction

Restriction of works performed by this Majlis Ash-Shura and not giving it a wider field to serve the country.
Confining works and discussions of Majlis Ash-Shura to what is referred to it by Majlis Ash-Shura of Ministers. It does not have the authority to select topics and issues to discuss.
Majlis Ash-Shura is not authorised to discuss important issues, such as the budget and security topics.
Deficiency of the political contribution of Majlis Ash-Shura in addition to the weakness of its capabilities in the issue of regulations.
Weakness of Majlis Ash-Shura resolutions, which in turn weakens Majlis Ash-Shura and reduces its credibility.
The suggestions made by Majlis Ash-Shura to the government are not executed.

Thus, the restriction of the works and authorities of Majlis Ash-Shura, the weakness of its jurisdiction and resolutions of Majlis Ash-Shura in regard of the general policy of the country is an obvious reason. One of the members expressed this by saying: "Majlis Ash-Shura is considered as an effective organisation in the process of making regulations and amending them, but its role in general politics needs to be widened and made more effective". This might be the cause why many of the members called for amendment of Majlis Ash-Shura regulations in a manner that gives it wider and stronger authority and jurisdiction to perform its mission in

119

the best way and to avoid its transformation from a political organisation into an institution of experts whose role is confined to revision and the amendment of regulations. One of the members stated this idea, arguing that: "The time has come to give Majlis Ash-Shura more authority and more power to enforce its resolutions". It is also vital to upgrade the status of Majlis Ash-Shura and give it more confidence to become a stronger organisation that supports the King and provide him with practical assistance".

Article 15 states that Majlis Ash-Shura has the right to express its opinion on the general policies of the State which are referred to it by the Prime Minister. In particular, it has the following functions:

1. To discuss and express its opinion on the general policy for social and economic development.
2. To study and suggest what is proper in relation to the Kingdom's rules, regulations, treaties, international accords and concessions.
3. To interpret regulations.
4. To discuss and offer suggestions relating to the annual reports submitted by the ministries and other government departments.

There are those who believe that the authorities and areas of specialisation granted to Majlis Ash-Shura by force of decreed law are too limited. In other words, its range of function is limited to issues referred to it by the Prime Minister. One of the members argues that Majlis Ash-Shura is not free to select an issue for discussion. Based on Article 23, a group of ten *Majlis Ash-Shura* members have the right to propose a topic of discussion but still that topic has to be approved by the King. He further argues that getting such an approval is a process that might take a long time, possibly years. This explains the reason why 11 members of those who had responded to the questionnaire called to have Article 23 activated or even amended. Along this approach, another member suggested that Majlis Ash-Shura resolutions should be considered final once approved by the King without recourse to the Council of Ministers. He argues that among the weakest points endured by Majlis Ash-Shura is that its resolutions are referred to the Council of Ministers. It is supposed, as he claimed, that Majlis Ash-Shura resolutions are final and should be adopted as effective regulations with the approval of the King. This is again a reference to Article 17. On the other hand there is another opinion that argues that time is still not ripe for such expansion or amendments. Majlis Ash-Shura is still in its early years of experience and there are other state issues that deserve priority of treatment. There is an pressing need, on the part of Majlis Ash-Shura, to meet such social needs before expanding the range of its authority e.g. revising laws and regulations that have been in effect for a long time. These laws and regulations have to be amended and new laws be enacted.

It is appropriate to provide solutions to the problems of Majlis Ash-Shura, to subsidise its requirements, and to increase its members and budget. Both the amendment of Articles and the elimination of obstacles can be addressed simultaneously but only after Majlis Ash-Shura's experience over the last two years has been evaluated. Based on the results of such an evaluation, certain mistakes can be avoided. This research study has proposed certain ideas that aim to develop Majlis Ash-Shura and improve its efficacy. We think that these ideas have to be accounted for upon considering the possibility of amending Majlis Ash-Shura regulatory system because they are initially taken from Majlis Ash-Shura members themselves.

7-18 Weakness of Managerial and Financial Capabilities

The study revealed that there are some managerial and financial difficulties that face Majlis Ash-Shura and the members. These difficulties hinder the development of work and prevent the utilisation of Majlis Ash-Shura capabilities in the best way. Some relevant examples referred to by members are indicated below:

Table 7.7 Weaknesses in Managerial and Financial Capabilities

Centralisation of management.
Delay of the Chairmanship of Majlis Ash-Shura in accepting suggestions.
Majlis Ash-Shura members are sometimes dealt with as employees and this of course has its drawbacks.
Tendency to cut costs.
The budget of Majlis Ash-Shura is low.
Majlis Ash-Shura does not bear the travel expenses of members who are residing out of Riyadh city, the headquarters of Majlis.
Weakness and inadequacies in the managerial system.
There is a long series of bureaucratic procedures when demanding the provision of simple matters.
Lack of experts and consultants to support both the administrative and executive systems.
Lack of flexibility in access to facilities for members requiring to perform work outside regular working hours.
Not exploiting all the capabilities and views of Majlis Ash-Shura members.

Such administrative and financial hindrances are a major obstacle in Majlis Ash-Shura's process of action. Therefore, these obstacles must be eliminated and Majlis Ash-Shura should be provided with all its financial needs and its administrative apparatus should be enhanced. There is a need to reconsider the methods adopted by Majlis Ash-Shura administration; a method other than centralisation should be adopted. The Vice-President of Majlis Ash-Shura, the General Secretary and the heads of the committees should be given further authority to conclude issues with reasonable speed and to minimise, as much as possible, all bureaucratic complications. This bureaucratic handicap was raised by one of the members, who claimed that whenever there is a need for a thing to be obtained or secured from one of Majlis Ash-Shura departments, an application to that effect has to be submitted to the head of Majlis Ash-Shura who in turn refers it to the General Secretary. He then finally submits it to the department concerned. Of course, in the concerned department there is a chain of bureaucratic procedures that are irrelevant and unhelpful.

In any department, the administration can play a central role and this is very true in the case of Majlis Ash-Shura as an important political institution. Hence, it is important to develop the administrative apparatus of Majlis Ash-Shura and provide it with experts and consultants so that the potentialities of Majlis Ash-Shura can be properly utilised. This is particularly true if we take into consideration the level of education and previous reliable experience of the members. Some of them are previous ministers, university rectors, army leaders, businessmen, physicians and university staff members and the like.

7-19 The Weakness of Interaction with Society

The outcomes of the study point out to the weakness of Majlis Ash-Shura interaction with and response to society and its needs. Moreover, a significant part of the population are not aware of the role of Majlis Ash-Shura, its authority and its works and activities. The following are some of the topics members have referred to by the members in this regard:

Table 7.8 Weaknesses in Interaction with Society

Majlis Ash-Shura does not publicise its work.
Many people are not aware of the role and activities of Majlis Ash-Shura.
Saudi society does not understand the nature of the work of Majlis Ash-Shura and its authority.
Some people confuse the organisational role of Majlis Ash-Shura and the tasks of executive governmental organisations.
Society has great expectations of Majlis Ash-Shura while it is not capable of achieving them in the light of its present authority.
A lack of sufficient interaction between Majlis Ash-Shura and the public.
The connection between Majlis Ash-Shura and the desires of citizens and

their suggestions (that are continuously sent), is broken, while many of these suggestions are in the public interest.
The credibility of Majlis Ash-Shura is shaken from the public's viewpoint.

One of the daily papers pointed out that Saudi public opinion and some analysts in the region blame members of Majlis Ash-Shura for not interacting with the vital issues and concerns of their society. Just a few examples are: the unemployment rate, the admission of secondary school graduates to colleges and universities, the non-employment of qualified youth, the existence of ancient regulations and governmental by-laws, the absence of discussion of the government budget, political, defence and security matters. Those who criticise Majlis Ash-Shura, blame the members for not taking an initiative to benefit from the content of Article 23 of Majlis Ash-Shura regulation that gives the right to any 10 members to draft a new regulation or an amendment to an existing one.

7-20 The Decline of Some Members' Participation in the Work of Majlis Ash-Shura

Despite the fact that the majority of members effectively participate in the works and activities of Majlis Ash-Shura, the outcome of the study has shown that the participation of some members is only formal and is ineffective. Also many of them are not entirely dedicated to Majlis Ash-Shura membership especially the businessmen. This is due to their commitments and obligations which might sometimes interfere with their obligations towards Majlis Ash-Shura.

Repeated reference has been made to the issue of some members' participation and their lack of dedication to the work of Majlis Ash-Shura. They considered this as one of the difficulties that confront them, as well as one of Majlis Ash-Shura points of weakness. One member said: "Work in Majlis Ash-Shura is routine-oriented, and the members' role is not as effective as it should be". Another member said: "The participation of some members is not as effective as it should be". Another member said: "I wish the participation of members was much more effective". "Some members are not participating in discussions, some are devoted to their own business and give less attention to Majlis Ash-Shura and the attendance of some members is only formal and done merely for the sake of attendance and not for effective participation". Another pointed out: "Many of Majlis Ash-Shura members are not dedicated to their membership".

Some of the members who are dedicated to Majlis Ash-Shura spoke of the contradiction of roles and referred to the load of their burdens and obligations. One member referred to the difficulties that he faces in "co-ordination between their work in Majlis Ash-Shura and other work in the private sector." Another defined the difficulty facing him saying: "My current work multiplies my commitments and obligations to Majlis Ash-Shura, where I am required to attend committee and Majlis Ash-Shura meetings two days a week".

The reducing level of some members' participation could be put down to a lack of dedication to Majlis Ash-Shura membership, the deficiency of support equipment and services, and adequate source of information in Majlis Ash-Shura

Majlis Ash-Shura's lack of interaction with the complaints and problems of the public is a fact that can not be ignored. However, this problem is initiated by the effect of Majlis Ash-Shura regulations, which limit the task of Majlis Ash-Shura and bind it to a specified range of action. The range of freedom of movement is provided as well as defined by Article 23. This right implied in Article 23 has not been utilised owing to the involvement of Majlis Ash-Shura in revising and amending old regulations and studying the numerous issues referred to it by the Prime Minister. The other fact is the low level of public awareness in the nature, activities and tasks delegated to Majlis Ash-Shura. Some people confuse the Consultative Majlis Ash-Shura and the regional Majlis Ash-Shura with the other government departments. This confusion is attributed to insufficient coverage by the media of the activities conducted by Majlis Ash-Shura.

7-21 Relations between Majlis and the Government
The outcome of the study points out a plurality of relations between Majlis Ash-Shura and the Council of Ministers, in addition to a lack of a specified tool for co-ordination between the two organisations. A member of Majlis Ash-Shura spoke of the need to define and clarify the relationship between Majlis Ash-Shura and the Council of Ministers. Another member spoke of the necessity of defining the relationship between Majlis Ash-Shura and the ruler. "The methods should be developed and improved", he argued.

The members mentioned many difficulties and points of weakness of the relationship to the government and its organisations. Among the difficulties are:
1. Accepting government suggestions without discussion.
2. Presenting resolutions of Majlis Ash-Shura to the Council of Ministers before being approved.
3. Shelving reports from the government to be studied and accounted for.

4. The weakness of the relationship of Majlis Ash-Shura with ministries and governmental organisations.
5. The inability of Majlis Ash-Shura to summon any minister directly for the purpose of consultation.
6. The sensitivity of some government officials toward Majlis Ash-Shura and the fact that they do not consider it seriously.

It is obvious that these points are important and they are indicative of the importance of the relationship between Majlis Ash-Shura and the Council of Ministers. More than one member has diagnosed the problem and prescribed the medication. They have argued that the blurred relationship between the two assemblies can be attributed to a lack of defined mechanism of co-ordination between the two. Therefore, the only solution is to create such a mechanism. Some members have already come up with certain suggestions pertinent to developing the relationship between the two entities (see the suggestions at the end of this chapter). It has been expected that Majlis Ash-Shura, being relatively new, might encounter problems and obstacles in the process of its interaction with the Council of Ministers and other Government Departments, in particular those that have not adapted to this new political institution. The same thing can be said about the way government officials view Majlis Ash-Shura. A scrutiny of the regulations relevant to the two Majlis Ash-Shuras would indicate an overlap in the areas of constitutionalism. The new regulations pertinent to the Council of Ministers, decreed by the King in 1994, mandate in addition to what is stipulated in "the state basic law" and in "the system of Majlis Ash-Shura", that the Council of Ministers shall be the government body that designs and plans the domestic, foreign, financial, economic, educational and defence policies of the Saudi State. In addition to overseeing all state public affairs, the Council of Ministers shall consider resolutions adopted by Majlis Ash-Shura. The regulation of the Council of Ministers did not explain how it is possible for the Council of Ministers to strike a balance between its domain and that of Majlis Ash-Shura. Moreover, the difference between "mandate" and "voice an opinion" is not made clear in the regulations of the two bodies. Article 15 of Majlis Ash-Shura dictates that Majlis Ash-Shura can express an opinion in the general policies of the State. Ashalhoob (1999) argued that it is obvious, that the Council of Ministers is given greater authority and effectiveness than that given to Majlis Ash-Shura mainly in the field of the constitution.

It is stipulated in the Saudi basic Law of Governance that the organisational authority shall exercise its authority based on this regulation and other regulations of the two entities. The organisational authority of the two bodies

126

is explained in the regulations of the Council of Ministers where its regulations mandate (with an observance of the regulations of Majlis Ash-Shura) that regulations, treaties, international accords, and concessions, shall be prepared and amended by the Council of Ministers. Basic to the conception of this approach, Majlis Ash-Shura of Ministers is considered an organisational body along with Majlis Ash-Shura (Ashalhoob, 1999).

Because of this overlap in the domains of the two councils, some of Majlis Ash-Shura members argue that among the weak points of Majlis Ash-

Shura is the vague relationship between the two bodies. What is required is to clear up this problem and, as a first step towards that end, the consultative nature of Majlis Ash-Shura appointment should be made clear. Is it a legislative body whose main function is to issue, study and amend regulations, or is it a political body, whose basic function is to voice opinions, present the King with advice whenever a need rises? Even though all articles depict Majlis Ash-Shura as an "organisational authority", still a scrutiny of its regulations would indicate that Majlis Ash-Shura is as close as possible to being a political institution. It advances advice and consultation. This approach is in itself the essence of Article 15 that defines the constituency of Majlis Ash-Shura and stipulates that "it presents opinions on issues referred to it by the Prime Minister pertinent to the general policy of the State". This means that the authorities of Majlis Ash-Shura are limited to the consideration of issues and regulations referred to it and consequently advance related opinions.

7-22 Difficulties Regarding Methods of Discussion and Decision-Making

The outcome of the study showed that there exist some points of weakness in Majlis Ash-Shura with difficulties confronting its members due to the manner of discussion and the process of decision-making. The major points of difficulties and weaknesses referred to by members are:

Table 7.9 Difficulties Regarding Methods of Discussion and Decision-Making

The domination of lower common denominator and a keenness to find solutions that please all. This approach reduces the necessary clarity of vision and prevents the crystallisation of defined attitudes.
What proceeds in discussions is not reflected in specific recommendations.

127

Not benefiting from the rich ideas expressed during sessions.
Slowness of Majlis Ash-Shura in developing a discussion procedure and a decision making process.
Members do not have the right of abstention during votes on resolutions.
The spending of much time in discussion.
The lengthy interventions by members during meetings.
Lack of reasoning of resolutions adopted by Majlis Ash-Shura and the brief explanation of backgrounds when conveying Majlis Ash-Shura point of view to other parties concerned.

Most of these problems can be justified on the ground that the experience of Majlis Ash-Shura is still limited and more time is needed to have its process of action, methods of deliberation and process of decision-making. Majlis Ash-Shura members have produced many suggestions on how to develop the procedural and organisational processes. They also suggested a possibility of Majlis Ash-Shura benefiting from the experience of other well-established Majlis Ash-Shura in the Muslim world. These suggestions are explained in detail in the course of the following discussions.

7-23 Absence of Advanced Notice of Agenda Prior to Sessions

The findings of the study revealed that delays in providing members with a work schedule of sessions, documents and topics for study are considered difficulties and barriers that hinder their process of work. Many of the members interviewed argued that this phenomenon is attributed to an inadequacy of time for members to study and collect data and be ready for discussion and the expression of opinions. This is particularly true mainly when the topic is one of vital issues that require extensive consideration.

7-24 Difficulties that Relate to Majlis Ash-Shura Regulations

The outcomes of the study showed that members of Majlis Ash-Shura are facing difficulties related to some articles of the regulation or its internal by-laws. One member suggested "insufficiency of time to study an issue at home is a decisive factor, which is due to the fact that, members are not allowed to take papers out of Majlis Ash-Shura premises". Another one said: "There exists an article that forbids the taking of documents out of Majlis Ash-Shura". This has been regarded as one of the difficulties and barriers that confront them in their work. The Article that deals with Majlis Ash-Shura regulation is Article 14 of the by-laws which states, "The member of Majlis Ash-Shura should study the schedule of work within the boundaries of Majlis Ash-Shura. A member is not allowed for any reason to take any papers, regulations, or documents that concern his work, outside Majlis Ash-Shura premises". The reason behind this is to maintain the confidentiality of topics, issues and documents studied by Majlis Ash-Shura. On the other hand, some members referred to "the plurality of vision in regard to dedication of the members and not allowing them to combine with work in Majlis Ash-Shura with other academic work such as lecturing". Reference here is made to Article 9 of the regulations. This article states: "It is not permitted to combine the membership of Majlis Ash-Shura with any governmental designation, or the management of any company, unless the King sees that there is a need for it."

This remark seems to have come from those university faculties that have been chosen for the membership of Majlis Ash-Shura. They like to give lectures even of a limited range because they feel that their roots are deeply connected to their scientific domain and their educational environment.

What is remarkable here is that Majlis Ash-Shura members are controversially different in respect to the members' dedication to work in Majlis Ash-Shura. Some of them see that there is a lack of dedication among members to the work and activities of Majlis Ash-Shura while others ask that the members should be permitted to practise other work in addition to working in Majlis Ash-Shura.

7-25 Other Difficulties

The responses of Majlis Ash-Shura members who answered the study questionnaire included some the following difficulties that confront them:

Table 7.10 Other Difficulties

Travelling weekly from their home to Riyadh city, where Majlis Ash-Shura is located, and returning home.
Lack of adaptation to the practices and discussions of Majlis Ash-Shura.
Monotony and weariness from lengthy sessions and meetings of Majlis Ash Shura.

From the above discussions proceeds the awareness that Majlis Ash-Shura is suffering many weaknesses and facing difficulties in performing its work and activities. These difficulties and aspects of weakness represent real barriers that hinder Majlis Ash-Shura from shouldering the responsibilities for which it was originally established. It appears that the major barriers that confront Majlis Ash-Shura and its members are the following:

1. Barriers represented by lack of equipment and information services.
2. Managerial and financial barriers, represented by the weakness of managerial and financial capabilities.
3. Social and informative barriers, represented by the weakness of interaction with the society and openness to information media.
4. Personal barriers, represented by the weakness of some members' participation in the works of Majlis Ash-Shura and its activities. This is added to a lack of dedication of many members to Majlis Ash-Shura membership.
5. Political barriers, represented by the plurality of the relationship between Majlis Ash-Shura on the one hand and the government on the other.
6. Disciplinary and procedural barriers in respect to the organisation sessions, meetings, manner of discussions and the process of decision-making.

These barriers require a careful scientific study, firstly, to define its causes, and secondly, to propose appropriate plans and methods to eliminate them. This could make Majlis Ash-Shura a strong and effective political organisation capable of supporting the ruler and providing him with proper opinions and mature scientific advice.

It is true that Majlis Ash-Shura has realised many tangible achievements during the short period of its existence which is not more than seven years. This has been accomplished despite the difficulties and barriers confronting Majlis Ash-Shura, and despite the limited experience of the members in handling problems with governmental organisations and other departments that are not accustomed to dealing with any entity other than the Council of Ministers.

An establishment of Majlis Ash-Shura as such is a kind of political development in the Kingdom of Saudi Arabia. The record of Majlis Ash-Shura is full of achievements and contributions to the state. The findings indicate that the accomplishments of Majlis Ash-Shura throughout the recent period have been concentrated on the issue and amendment of a number of regulations, by-laws, treaties and agreements. This has had a positive effect in the process of development in the Kingdom and on the improvement of services rendered to citizens to cope with the requirements of modern age.

It is evident that Majlis Ash-Shura has suffered some points of weakness and confronted some barriers. The most significant of these barriers are the weakness of supportive services, the lack of equipment and information, the limited authority and jurisdiction, and the weakness of financial and administrative capabilities. In contrast, Majlis Ash-Shura has many positive aspects and points of strength, such as: dependency on the Kurān and Al Sunna of the Prophet, high effectiveness in performing its tasks, varied membership background, freedom of opinion during sessions, openness and objectiveness during discussions, dominance of public interest and an absence of party, group, or regional affiliation or coalitions.

An objective assessment of Majlis Ash-Shura over the recent period reveals merits that outweigh its negative aspects.

It would be hard to find a more accurate statement to evaluate Majlis Ash-Shura than the opinion expressed by a Majlis Ash-Shura member:

> "Majlis Ash-Shura is considered to be an effective organisation in the process of regulation and amendment. Still, Majlis Ash-Shura can play greater role towards the amendment of its by-laws."

7-26 Recommendations to Develop Majlis Ash-Shura and Increase its Effectiveness

As this study tries to trace the problems, barriers, and points of weakness of Majlis Ash-Shura, it also tries to find solutions and suggestions to solve these problems. Since members of Majlis Ash-Shura are best able to diagnose the problems of Majlis Ash-Shura itself and the obstacles that confront it, and to define its needs, they are also the most capable of providing solutions for these problems. The researcher has been very keen to include the following question in the questionnaire that was handed to members of Majlis Ash-Shura: "In your opinion, how can Majlis Ash-Shura be improved as far as

its performance and mechanisms are concerned"? Their suggestions were classified into twelve categories as shown in Table 7.11.

131

Table 7.11 Suggestions to Develop Majlis Ash-Shura and Increase its Level of Effectiveness

No	Suggestion	Freq.
1.	Support equipment, support services, the development of information resources.	19
2.	Expanding the authority and jurisdiction of Majlis	16
3.	Creation of new committees	16
4.	Development of the administrative and executive systems	13
5.	Article 23 of Majlis regulations. Amending and enforcing	11
6.	The interaction of and strengthening of relationships with society.	10
7.	Increasing the membership and their dedication to the work of Majlis.	10
8.	Elaboration and development the relationship between Majlis and the government.	9
9.	Developing the foundation of work and organisational procedures.	8
10.	Conduct of studies for the assessment and development of Majlis	4
11.	Support Majlis budget and financial capabilities.	3
12.	Other miscellaneous suggestions	5

Table 7.11 itemises the suggestions of Majlis Ash-Shura members to develop Majlis Ash-Shura and increase its level of performance and effectiveness. It is clear from the outcomes shown in this table that supporting equipment, services and information, in addition to expanding authorities and jurisdiction of Majlis Ash-Shura by the creation of new committees and developing the administrative and executive systems, and enforcing Article 23 of Majlis Ash-Shura regulation and amending it can all improve the performance of Majlis Ash-Shura. This might be attributed to the fact that the difficulties and points of weakness of Majlis Ash-Shura are centred in these areas. These aspects are important to the progress of Majlis Ash-Shura and to improving its ability to perform its tasks.

From the information in table 7.11, it can be argued that there is a need on the part of Majlis Ash-Shura to interact with society, increase the dedication of the members and strengthen its relationship with the government. There is also a need to support its budget and financial capabilities. This research provides practical suggestions along this line to be discussed at the end of this chapter.

7-27-1 Expanding the Authority and Jurisdiction of Majlis

The results of this research study have shown that the first important suggestion presented by Ash-Shura members to develop the efficacy of Majlis Ash-Shura is to expand the range of Majlis Ash-Shura's authority and provide Majlis Ash-Shura resolutions with greater force. This suggestion was emphasised in the responses received from sixteen members. The second difficulty in the range of weakness is related to the parochialism of Majlis Ash-Shura authority.

In order to increase the range of *Ash-Shura* authorities, the members advanced suggestions and opinions that can be classified as follows:

1. To expand the scope of the jurisdiction and responsibilities of Majlis Ash-Shura and give it more legal jurisdiction to be able to promote the interests of the country and cope with the requirements of current times.
2. To increase Majlis Ash-Shura's involvement in studying the important and fundamental issues. To design general policies of the state and review the annual budget and issues, such as security, defence and foreign policy.
3. To give Majlis Ash-Shura the authority to question officials suspected of committing violations or abuses of authority.
4. To give direct right to Majlis Ash-Shura to study and discuss issues and topics which the majority of members deem as crucial and to advance related solutions and recommendations view.

133

5. Provide Majlis Ash-Shura resolutions with greater force so that they can become effective provided the King approves them – without any recourse to the Council of Ministers.

It is obvious that taking these suggestions into consideration would demand an amendment to Majlis Ash-Shura regulations. The question to be raised at this point of analysis is "Is the time now ripe to amend the regulations of Majlis Ash-Shura in this way"? We have seen that 16 members of those who responded to the questionnaire are in favour of an expansion of Majlis Ash-Shura's authority. One of them even argued that the time has come to provide Majlis Ash-Shura with a greater range of authority and enhance its resolutions. Other members argue that Majlis Ash-Shura is still young, which is why they believe that the time has not yet come to conduct such amendments. They also argue that there are other imperative matters worthy of discussion by Majlis Ash-Shura. It seems an evaluation of previous experience is essential so that all negative practices can be avoided and all the appropriate administrative techniques can be provided.

7-27-2 Creation of New Committees

Some members see a need to have new committees established. This approach can be analysed as follows:

1   Suggestions of members in this aspect are centred upon the distribution of responsibilities in the areas of education, culture and information affairs. Such members argue that the committees concerned can each be split into two committees. They call for separate committees for cultural and information affairs. The majority of the members who support the formation of new committees made this suggestion.

2   To divide the responsibilities of the Economic and Finance Committees into two committees by establishing a separate committee for financial affairs.

3   To establish a committee for planning and budget responsible for the discussion of the annual budget and state development plans. This committee is would also be concerned with environmental issues as well as the long term plans, strategies and future studies.

4   To separate the services and public utilities into two committees.

5   To create a functional multi-speciality committee for development. This committee should be responsible for (1) the co-ordination between various committees, (2) study issues of a common nature, follow up research on certain study methods tailored to develop Majlis Ash-Shura and its internal procedures.

A proposal for new committees 16 times in the responses received from the members. This percentage is indicative of the importance of having specialised committees in Majlis Ash-Shura. It seems that such committees can play a major supporting role in performing the tasks of Majlis Ash-Shura. These committees and the experts working in them perform a precise scrutiny of issues referred to Majlis Ash-Shura. The reports advanced by these committees help Majlis Ash-Shura to pass appropriate resolutions.

A committee to handle collected data might be named the "Information and Communication Committee". Most proposals support the division of some committees into two committees with the tasks halved between them. This approach can be understood given the excessive workload. In this regard, one of the members argued that some committees have workloads that exceed their capabilities. This explains why there is a need to reallocate their duties and assign some of the duties to new committees. Another member claimed that there are committees that have a workload that hardly requires the formation of such a committee, while there are numbers of substantial tasks left without designated committees. What is proper here is to reconsider the number and numbers of the specialisation of the committees and design a solution based on the demands of the task.

One of the members expressed a different opinion: he argued that it has been decided that eight committees should be established even though there seems no need for any additional committee.

The results of this research have shown that 43% of those who responded to the questionnaire see a need for more committees while 57% do not admit that need. The important committees recommended by the members to be established are:

1.   A committee for culture and mass media.
2.   A committee for financial affairs.
3.   A communication and information committee.

It seemed that Majlis Ash-Shura adopted the above resolution and admitted that the load of the appointment demands the formation of specialised

135

committees along with new ones. This approach is adopted based on Article 23 of Majlis Ash-Shura by-laws. It stipulates that "Majlis Ash-Shura is authorised to dissolve its committees and appoint new ones". On October 4, 1999, a few months after the completion of our survey, Majlis Ash-Shura decided on the formation of three committees (Resolution No. 17/60/6); the total number of the committees increased to eleven. The three new committees are the same committees considered in the results of this research study. Even the names of the first two have been given to the committees noted in the results. The exception is the third one, whose name was proposed by Majlis Ash-Shura to be slightly different: "the Shipment and Transportation Committee". The services rendered by this committee used to be conducted by the Public Services Committee. Due both to the important role played by the specialised committees, and to the demands of the constantly changing tasks, it is expected that the committees will continue to be restructured to meet the demands of prospective change, especially, if the members of Majlis Ash-Shura are to be increased in number and the range of their duties to be expanded.

7-27-3 Development of the Administrative and Executive System

In order to revive its role in building state institutions, Majlis Ash-Shura has laid down the bases of the procedures needed to realize this goal. This

approach was done by way of certain rules and modern regulations, the purpose of which is to have tasks completed within Majlis Ash-Shura. During its first year, Majlis Ash-Shura concentrated on building supporting departments and harmonising national qualifications for members, as well as training and acquainting its members and employees with the nature of Majlis Ash-Shura's role. Al Muhana (1998) argues that Majlis Ash-Shura designed plans to train its employees and develop their job performance. It seems that Majlis Ash-Shura still needs to develop its organisational structure based on its experience throughout the previous years. This approach emphasises the conclusion that the third important point of weakness endured by Majlis Ash-Shura lies in a problem related to administrative and financial factors. This is why the suggestion for the development of the administrative and executive body falls in the fourth rank of suggestions proposed by Majlis Ash-Shura members as a means to develop the efficacy and performance of Majlis Ash-Shura. Based on opinions related to the question of development derived from Majlis Ash-Shura members, the following guidelines were decided upon:

136

1. To support the administrative and executive system of Majlis Ash-Shura with the necessary equipment and manpower that are capable of performing the administrative work required.
2. The adoption of a decentralised style in the management of Majlis Ash-Shura affairs and work, together with giving further authorities to the Vice-President and the Secretary General to expedite work and enhance administrative performance.
3. To complete the administrative and technical system of Majlis Ash-Shura and give priority to specialised committees and support them with technical staff.

It is obvious that suggestions of this nature are very important for a political institution such as Majlis Ash-Shura, which is unlike any other government department.

Basic to the fact that most of Majlis Ash-Shura members are highly educated with considerable previous experience with government departments, it can be argued that the administration and handling of their affairs require a special mechanism, which needs to be different from any mechanism observed in any other government department.

This fact demands constant development of the apparatus of Majlis Ash-Shura. There is also a need to modernise its administrative mechanism to reach a level that suits the nature of Majlis Ash-Shura and the background of its members. The basic law has provided Majlis Ash-Shura with a freedom that can not be subjected to any outside supervision. Through this freedom Majlis Ash-Shura can set up regulations and procedures that can contribute to the realisation of its objectives. Based on this permitted freedom, Majlis Ash-Shura can conduct all necessary measures pertinent to matters of finance without recourse to any government department. This authority is based on both Article 29 of Majlis Ash-Shura system and Article 34 of its by-laws. According to Al Muhana (1998), this freedom has allowed Majlis Ash-Shura to set up its regulations and procedures and consequently to achieve them. To have these procedures and regulations developed, there is a need to conduct a constant revision to bring them to the proper level of progress. In administrating Majlis Ash-Shura affairs, it is obvious that Majlis Ash-Shura members assign a special importance to designated committees. These committees are viewed as a laboratory where the initial studies on the issues referred to it are conducted and tentative drafting of any regulation to be adopted are also planned. This makes imperative overall comprehensive support of all aspects of the committees.

7-27-4 Amendment of Article 23 of Majlis Ash-Shura Regulations

Article 23 of Majlis Ash-Shura regulations states: "A group of 10 members of Majlis Ash-Shura has the right to suggest a project of a new regulation or amendment of a valid regulation and present it to the President of Majlis Ash-Shura. The President of Majlis Ash-Shura should present the proposal to the King".

To activate this article and increase the effectiveness of Majlis Ash-Shura and expand its abilities, the members have suggested a range of proposals that can be summarised as follows:

1. To stimulate the spirit of initiation among Majlis Ash-Shura members to the benefit of this article by introducing constructive ideas and proposals in regard to regulations.
2. To amend this article to become positive so that time is saved in a manner that makes it more inclusive and gives a wider field for members to put forward ideas and suggestions.
3. To give the right to each member to suggest a study that he may find appropriate for Majlis Ash-Shura. The topics approved by Majlis Ash-Shura shall be referred to the specialised committees for study and then presented to Majlis Ash-Shura for discussion and recommendation before forwarding it to the King. Majlis Ash-Shura should not be confined only to discuss issues that are referred to it by the Council of Ministers.

4. To benefit from the content of this article, members are encouraged to take any initiative to study important issues, discuss the common problems of society and the issues that concern public opinion. They can suggest appropriate solutions, before referring the matter to the King.
5. To establish a committee for planning and future studies. This committee shall be concerned with short-term plans and long-term strategies. It can concern itself with the effectiveness of Article 23 of Majlis Ash-Shura regulations and use it in tackling future issues, particularly the future of the developmental sector.

As-Shalhoob (1999) argued, while basic to Article 23, ten members of Majlis Ash-Shura can collectively propose a new law or amend an effective one. It seems two implied factors have curtailed this right: (1) it is mandated that what the members can suggest should be confined to the area of "regulation"; (2) Whatever

138

the members suggest should be submitted to the head of Majlis Ash-Shura, who in his turn transfers it to the King. This means that Majlis Ash-Shura cannot consider any proposal submitted by the ten members unless and until it has been approved by the King. This process might involve a long time and complicated procedures. This is why Majlis Ash-Shura members emphasise that Article 23 should be amended so that Majlis Ash-Shura becomes authorised to study and consider issues and matters related to suggestions advanced by a quorum of ten Majlis Ash-Shura members and finally present its recommendation on this matter to the King.

Awaiting the proposed amendment of Article 23 to be passed, Majlis Ash-Shura members propose that Majlis Ash-Shura should benefit from this Article and advance constructive opinions pertinent to amendment regulations of and continue studying important issues and problems that prevail in Saudi society. The members' concern with Article 23 has become so strong that a member of Majlis Ash-Shura has suggested that a committee should be established to: (1) activate this article, (2) consider long term plans, and (3) make use of the implication of Article 23 to handle future related matters. Other members of

Majlis Ash-Shura suggested that the number of Majlis Ash-Shura sessions should be increased with greater efforts exerted by Majlis Ash-Shura members to activate Article 23. The great concern of members with Article 23 is justified on the ground that the authority and leverage of Majlis Ash-Shura is limited because Article 23 can provide Majlis Ash-Shura with additional open leverage. Accordingly, the members suggested that the article should be activated.

7-27-5 The Strengthening of Relations with Society

The results of the study have shown that among the most salient obstacles and the eminent points of weakness endured by Majlis Ash-Shura are: (1) inactivity on the part of Majlis Ash-Shura to deal and respond to the desires, expectations and other prospects of Saudi society and (2) the public's low awareness of the nature and activities of Majlis Ash-Shura. Based on this analysis it has been expected that a development of Majlis Ash-Shura and its mechanism and an increase in the level of interaction between Majlis Ash-Shura and society might come at the top of Majlis Ash-Shura members' list of priorities. Among the salient points proposed by members are:

1. To enforce informative openness of Majlis Ash-Shura to the extent of permiting media coverage of its activities. This may include direct broadcasting of sessions or at least broadcasting them later to increase the awareness of the public.

2. To increase the relationship between Majlis Ash-Shura and citizens. There is a need for intensive education programs to increase the awareness and understanding of the citizens of the nature of Majlis Ash-Shura, its works, and basic missions.
3. To open channels of communication with people on issues studied by Majlis Ash-Shura before voting.
4. To strengthen the relationship of Majlis Ash-Shura with society and its private organisations and increase its interaction with people in addition to exploring their expectations, worries and problems.

The criticism directed to Majlis Ash-Shura for being inactive in its interaction with the needs, problems, and critical issues of Saudi society is directed against upon the limited authority given to Majlis Ash-Shura. It is also attributed the fact that many members do not work full time in Majlis Ash-Shura. They busy themselves with personal matters. It is obvious that suggestions advanced by the members in this regard are important, practical and should be taken into consideration. An article published by Majlis Ash-Shura (1999) indicated that is interested in strengthening its interactions with Saudi citizens, establishing channels of communication with them keeping them aware of the process of this work and soliciting their opinions on matters that concern them. This approach has been applied through a number of channels, such as:

1. Soliciting opinions from citizens and studying them. This task has been entrusted to the Petition Committee, which is an administrative body within Majlis Ash-Shura instituted as a result of a decision by the Head of Majlis Ash-Shura. This committee is a liaison between Majlis Ash-Shura and the citizens.
2. Majlis Ash-Shura has made special arrangements by means of which citizens can visit it and acquaint themselves with its utilities and equipment. They can get direct answers to their questions from Majlis Ash-Shura officials.
3. According to Al Muhanna (1998), Majlis Ash-Shura has been interested in getting feedback from experts and specialists on issues that concern social sectors.

It seems that even the channels discussed above still need to be further activated. There is a need to develop as well as to strengthen the feeling, on the part of the citizens, that Majlis Ash-Shura is directly concerned with their problems and expectations. This feeling, with most Saudi citizens, is still limited.

140

7-27-5 Increased Membership and Dedication of Members to the Work of Majlis Ash-Shura

At the present time, Majlis Ash-Shura is composed of 90 members in addition to the Chairman. They are men of knowledge, both learned and experienced. The king selects them but each one should exhibit the following characteristics. He should be:

1. A Saudi national in terms of origin and by birth.
2. Renowned for being well qualified and of good reputation.
3. Not less than 30 years old.

Ten members included in their responses suggestions concerning the number of members and ways and standards of appointing them and their dedication to membership. The most important proposals in this regard:

1. To increase Majlis Ash-Shura members in the manner that makes it proportional to the size of the population of the Kingdom.
2. To give more attention to the standards of members' selection; to expand the representation of the careers and business sector in Majlis Ash-Shura with those who fulfil the conditions of scientific specialisation, experience and age.
3. To study the possibility of selection from a shortlist approved by the regional Majlis Ash-Shura.
4. Dedication of members to Majlis Ash-Shura so that work can be completed faster. One member suggested that the possibility of combining Majlis Ash-Shura membership with some limited academic activities which do not conflict with Majlis Ash-Shura work. Their heavy work load and the numerous responsibilities that they have to shoulder is a good enough reason to call for an increase Majlis Ash-Shura members. Majlis Ash-Shura members should work full-time and should be selected from different important developing social sectors, so that Majlis Ash-Shura can perform its duties perfectly and without delay.

In its initial state, Majlis Ash-Shura comprised 60 members in addition to the Head of Majlis Ash-Shura. Six years later, in 1998, the number was increased to 90 members. Still the present Majlis Ash-Shura argues that the number of the members is insufficient and suggests that it could be increased to between 100 and 200. A member of Majlis Ash-Shura has justified this call for an increase by claiming that more members would allow Majlis Ash-Shura resolutions to reflect the prevalent trends in Saudi society and would make any external influence, that might be exercised by the government, businessmen, or any beneficiary, less likely.

In contrast to this approach, there are those who do not see a need for such an increase. On the contrary, a group of members wish to have the number reduced. In this regard a member of proponents of this approach has argued that "sixty members, as it was the case in the first term of Majlis Ash-Shura, can handle all its affairs." The author thinks that the present number can be quite efficient and there is no need for any addition of members.

7-27-6 Elaboration and Development of Majlis Ash-Shura's Relationship with the Government

The three new regulations decreed in Saudi Arabia (the State Basic Law of Government, the System of Majlis Ash-Shura and the System of the Council of Ministers) have established a strong relationship between Ash-Shura and the Council of Ministers. The results of this research study indicate that this vague relationship is one of the most salient difficulties endured by Majlis Ash-Shura. (This point was discussed above). Accordingly, it has been natural and expected to see Majlis Ash-Shura Members suggest that the relationship between the two bodies should be made clear. They claim that in order to improve and develop the efficacy of Majlis Ash-Shura, this relationship should be clarified. Some of Majlis Ash-Shura members mentioned different suggestions in this respect:

1. To develop a relationship tool between Majlis Ash-Shura and the Council of Ministers. There is a need to establish effective communication channels with other systems.
2. The creation of a ministerial portfolio for Majlis Ash-Shura affairs that can act as a link between the Council of Ministers and Majlis Ash-Shura in place of paper dealings.
3. To appoint a member of Majlis Ash-Shura of State Minister status to attend the meetings of the Council of Ministers and its public corporation and to press the opinion of Majlis Ash-Shura in issues common to both.
4. The participation of the government in the sessions of Majlis Ash-Shura through attendance of the Ministers and officials to these sessions when issues are under discussion that relate to their ministries. Each ministry or entity should have a representative in attending sessions.
5. To specify a body that can follow up the adherence of government organisations and departments to the resolutions and recommendations taken by Majlis Ash-Shura and approved by the King.

These points are important and putting them into effect would improve the relationship between Majlis Ash-Shura and the government apparatus, mainly the Ministries. This relationship should be defined and advanced to help in achieving and facilitating the tasks that are shared by the two entities. This approach might require certain amendments to be carried out on the regulatory system of both Majlis Ash-Shura and the Council of Ministers. There might be a need to develop the mechanism of the relationship between the two bodies and provide Majlis Ash-Shura with further authorities and enhance its resolutions. In other words, it is a call that Majlis Ash-Shura might be given a greater range of independence the way it administers its affairs and the way it selects its in topics of discussion. There is a need to eliminate the overlap in areas of specialities between the two entities, because this overlap is considered a direct cause of the vagueness in the relationship between them.

7-27-7 Development of the Work Basis and the Disciplinary Procedures

The by-laws of Majlis Ash-Shura have defined the number of regular sessions of Majlis Ash-Shura, the way the agenda should be prepared, distributed to the members, and the methods of deliberations in the sessions. The General Commission of Majlis Ash-Shura has issued a list of rules that should be observed to have its work, tasks and other committees well organised. These regulations and rules are fully observed in the processes of Majlis Ash-Shura. The results of the research study indicate that the problems encountered by the members are related to the method of discussion, the process of decision making, the agenda and matters related to the rules of action exercised in Majlis Ash-Shura. Concerning this phenomenon, Majlis Ash-Shura members have suggested that the procedural methods and rules should be reconsidered and developed. It is obvious that these suggestions are important, for they are directly related to practical matters. It is argued that the achievement of such approach would enable the members to execute their works easily and smoothly and it would save them time and improve the quality of their performance. It is obvious that to execute suggestions number 2, 3 and 4, there is a need to amend certain items in the list of effective performance rules. It seems that the first suggestion is extremely important for it implies a utilisation of the experience of other noted Majlis Ash-Shura in the Muslim world. A utilisation of the good aspects of the experience of others would help to develop the rules and functional mechanisms of Majlis Ash-Shura. Thus the pitfalls and bad experiences of others need not be repeated.

The second suggestion is important simply because an agenda advanced to the members before a proposed session means that they would have enough time to study fully and consider all the issues..

The members' suggestions in this regard could be summed up as follows:

1. Imitating the experience of some firmly established Majlis Ash-Shuras in other countries and reflecting on their experience in the development of work. This would be particularly effective in regard to the steps of studying topics referred to Majlis Ash-Shura, the ways of discussing it and making related decisions, the schedule of the distribution of sessions and the role of the committee in Majlis Ash-Shura.
2. Circulating work schedule, agenda, information and documents of issues in ample time before sessions are held.
3. Permiting members to take out of Majlis Ash-Shura, papers and documents regarding their work and conduct a complete study on them and prepare their arguments. Members should be allowed to come to their offices at Majlis Ash-Shura at any time to complete their assignments.
4. Defining the number of interventions and confine them to no more than five minutes in addition to taking necessary action that might help to save time. The concentration of speech and optimum utilisation of the time devoted for the session. The Chairman should intervene whenever he deems necessary.
5. Summarising Majlis Ash-Shura deliberations and discussions and attach them to any related topic under discussion.
6. Amending Article II of the rules of Majlis Ash-Shura and committees. This article states that "Any member should participate in voting either by approval or disapproval". There should be a third choice, i.e. abstention.
7. Specifying topics of priority and importance, and expedite their preparation while giving them the time they deserve in discussion.

Selected Bibliography

Abdel Wassie, A.A. Wahab, (1970) *Education in Saudi Arabia*, MacMillan, London.

Abdul Hafiz, A. Fathi (1996) *Legitimacy of Authority in Islam: A Comparative Study.* Alexandria – House of New University, (Arabic).

Abu-Eid, A. (1989) *Sovereignty in Islam: a Contrastive Research.* Al-Manar Library, Zarka, Jordan, (Arabic).

Ahmad Kamal, A.M. (1991) *A Contemporary Islamic Vision: An Announcement of Principles,* Dar al Shuruq, Cairo, p.6.

Al Awa, M.S. (1989) *The Political System of the Saudi States,* 1st edition, Dar Ash-Shorooq, Cairo, pp.150-180.

Al Awaji, I.M. (1971) *Bureaucracy and Society in Saudi Arabia.* Woodrow Wilson Department of Government and Foreign Affairs, University of Virginia, Charlottesville, Virginia, unpublished Ph.D. dissertation.

Al Awani, T.J. (1994) *Source Methodology in Islamic Jurisprudence, (Usul Al Fiqh Al Islami),* International Institute of Islamic Thought, Herndon, pp.12-15.

Al Baz, A. (1998) *The Political and Constitutional System in the Kingdom of Saudi Arabia.* Dar Al-Khoraiji, Riyadh, (Arabic).

Al Duraib, S.S. (1984) *The Foundation of the Judiciary and its Applications in Saudi Arabia,* Dar Al Elm Press, Jeddah.

Al Gazzali, I.M. (1971) *Tawhid and Tawakkal (Oneness of God and Dependence Upon God),* cited in: *The Book of Constructive Virtues (Ihya Ulum Id Din),* Vol.4, Part 1, F.K. Islami Mission Trust, Dacca, pp.235-296.

Al Hamad, T. (1986) *Towhid Al Jazira Al Arabia dawr Al Idiulyjiyya Wa Al Tanthim fitahtim Al bunya Al ijtimaiyya Al Iqtisadiyya Al Mu'iqa lilwahda (The Unification of the Arabian Peninsula: The Role of Ideology and Organisation in Overcoming the Socio-economic Structure Preventing Unity),* Al Mustaqbal Al Arabi, Vol.93, November.

Al Hayat, March 2, 1997, P 6 – The text of the King's speech can be found.

Al Johany, E.M. (1992) *Consultation and the Art of Government in the Kingdom of Saudi Arabia.* King Su'ud University Press. Riyadh.

Al Mana, M. (1980) *Arabia Unified, A Portrait of Ibn Su'ud.* Hutchinson Benham Ltd., London.

Al Mohanna, M. (1999) *A Record of Ash-Shura Activities* (First Term), Press and Public Relations Department, Riyadh, p.93.

Almond G. and Coleman. Jr. 1960 Politics of the Developing areas, Princeton University Press, New Jersey.

Almond, Gabriel and G. Bingharn Powell Jr. 1978, Comparative Politics: Systems, Process, And Policy, Boston: Little Brown.

Al Muhanna, M. (1999) *Records of Public Administration,* Ash-Shura Circulation Press, Riyadh.

Al Najjar, M. R. (1991) "Contemporary Trends in the Study of Folklore in the Arab Gulf States", in: Davis and Gavrielides, *Statecraft in the Middle East,* pp.176-201.

Needler, Martin C. Political Development in Latin America: Instability, Violence and Evolutionary Change. 1968. New York: Random House.

Nyroap, Richard F. 1977. Area Handbook For Saudi Arabia. Washington DC Department of Defense.

Al Othaimeen, A. (1995) *The Wars of King Abdul Aziz to Unite the Kingdom,* Riyadh, (Arabic).

Al Qassimi, T. (1990) *Government System in Shari'a and Islamic History.* 6th edition, Dar An-nafais, Beirut, pp.66-75.

Al Rihani, A. (1978) *A History of Najd & Annexed Territory and the Story of Abdul Aziz.* 4th edition, Dar Rihani, Beirut, (Arabic).

Al Rihani, A. (1981) *History of Najd and its Territories.* 4th edition, Al Fakhriyah Beirut Press, Beirut.

Al Rihani, A. (1983) *The Makers of Modern Arabia.* Greenwood Press, New York, p.238.

Al Shaer, A. (1991) *Kingdom of Saudi Arabia History, Civilization and Development (60 years of progress),* Ministry of Information, Riyadh, (Arabic).

Al Shalhoub, A.R. (1991) *The Constitutional System in Saudi Arabia between Islamic Shari'a and Comparative Laws,* pp.22-32, (Arabic).

Al Sweel, A.I. and Wright, J.W. Jr. (eds.), *Saudi Arabia, Tradition and Transition,* The Saudi Arabia Cultural Mission, Washington, D.C.

Al Torki, S. and Cole, D. (1989) *Arabian Oasis City: The Transformation of Unayzah.* University of Texas Press, Austin, Texas.

Al Yasseen, A. *Majlis Ash-Shura Al-Saudi: Tajrobah raedah. (Saudi Majlis Ash-Shura: A leading experience.* In: Al Khaleej *Al-Arabi Wa Afaq Al-Koran Al-Ishreen.* Mohammed Al-Romaihi, Kuwait, p.24, (Arabic).

Al Yassini, A. (1985) *Religion and State in the Kingdom of Saudi Arabia.* Westview Press, Boulder, Colorado, pp.68-72, 76.

Al Zahrani, A.R. (1999) *Maseerat Majlis Ash-Shura in al-Mamlakah Al-Arabiayah Al-Saudia (The Progress of Majlis Ash-Shura in the Kingdom of Saudi Arabia),* Riyadh, p.547, (Arabic).

Almond, G. and Coleman, J. (1960) *The Politics of the Developing Areas.* Princeton University Press, Princeton, New Jersey.

146

Anderson, L. (1991) "Abolutism and Resilience of Monarchy in the Middle East", *Political Science Quarterly*, Vol.106, No.1.

Annadi, F. (1999) *The Principles of the Government System in Islam*, 2nd edition, Dubai Police College, Dubai, pp.140-195.

As Shalboonb, A. A. (1999) *The Constitutional System in the Kingdom of Saudi Arabia Between Shari'a and Comparative Law*. Al-Shegry Press House, Riyadh, p.244.

Assah, A. (1969) *The Miracle of the Desert Kingdom*: Johnson Publications Ltd., London, (Arabic).

Brog, W.R. & Gall, M.D. (1989) *Educational Research*, 5th edition, Longman, New York.

Browman, J. S. (1986) *Administration and Development in the Arab World*. Garland Publishing Inc., New York.

Binder, Leonard. 1971 Crises and Sequences in Political Development Princeton. New Jersey : Princeton University Press.

Bill, James A. 1981. Comparative Politics: The Quest For Theory. Washington Dc. University Press of America.

Chaudhury, K.A. (1989) The Prince of Wealth: Business and State in Labor Remittance and Oil Economies, *International Organization*, Vol.43, No.1, pp.137-140.

Cleron, J.P, (1978) *Saudi Arabia 2000: A Strategy for Growth*, St. Martin's Press, New York.

Cole, P. D. (1975) *Nomads of the Nomads: The Al Murrah Bedouin of the Empty Quarter*. AHM Publishing Corporation, Arlington Heights, Illinois, pp.146-163.

Crystal, J. (1990) *Oil and Politics in the Gulf: Rulers and Merchants in Kuwait and Qatar*, Cambridge University Press, New York, Chapters 2, 3 and 5.

Dahlan, A.H. (1990) *Politics, Administration and Development in Saudi Arabia*. Dar Al Shoroug, Jeddah.

Daiber, H. (1993) Political Philosophy, in: *A History of Islamic Philosophy*, Part II, Nasr and Leaman (eds.), Arayeh Cultural Institute, Tehran, pp.841.

Davis, E. (1991) Theorising Statecraft and Social Change in the Arab Oil Producing Countries. In: Davis, E. and Gaverielides, N. (eds.), *Statecraft in the Middle East: Oil, Historical Memory and Popular Culture*. Florida International University Press, Miami, Florida, p.13.

Doumato, E. (1991) *Women and the Stability of Saudi Arabia,* Middle East Report, No.171, July/August, pp.34-37.

Eickelman, D.E. (1984) *Kings and People: Oman's State Consultative Council* Middle East Journal, Vol.38, No.1. pp.51-71.

Eickelman, D.E. (1989*) National Identity and Religious Discourse in Contemporary Oman,* International Journal of Islamic and Arabic Studies, Vol.6, No.1.

Eisenstandt, S.N. Building State And nations, 1973. Beverly Hills.

Encyclopaedia of Seerah (1998) *Establishment of Justice,* Encyclopaedia of Seerah, Vol.III, Seerah Foundation, London, pp.257-283.

Fadlallah M.H. (1990) *The Islamic Movement: Issues and Concerns,* Dar al Malak, Beirut, p.10.

Fuller, G., (1999) *Political Islam and U.S. Policy,* Middle East Affairs Journal, Vol.5, Winter/Spring, pp147-160.

Harrington, C.W. (1958) *The Saudi Arabian Council of Ministers, Middle East Journal,* Vol.12.

Heard B.F. (1982) *From Trucial States to United Arab Emirates.* Longman, New York, Chapter 2.

Helms, C.M. (1981) *The Cohesion of Saudi Arabia,* Johns Hopkins University Press, Baltimore, Chapters 1,3 and 8.

Hippler and Lueg, (1995) *The Next Threat: Western Perceptions of Islam,* Pluto Press, Boulder, Colorado.

Hippler and Lueg (1999) *Twenty Years of Islamic Politics, Bullet,* The Middle East Journal, Vol.53, No.2, Spring, pp.187-200.

Holden, D. & Johns, R. (1981). *The House of Su'ud, The Rise and Rule of the Most Powerful Dynasty.* Holt, Rinehart and Winston, New York. pp.10-35.

Huntington, S. (1993) *The Clash of Civilisations,* Foreign Affairs, Vol.72, No.3, Summer, pp.22-49.

Huntington, Samuel. 1968. Political Order in Changing Societies. Yale University Press : New Haven.

Ibn Bishr, A.O. (1982) *Title of Glory in the History of Najd.* Part 1 Darat Al-Malak Abdul Aziz Press, (Arabic).

Iqbal, M. (1986) *Saudi Arabia, Its Founding and Development,* Jagowal Printing Press, Kashmir, pp.52-59.

Jaeger, R.M. (1983) *Statistics: A Spectator Sport.* Sage Publications, Beverly Hills, California.

James, B. (1984) *Resurgent Islam in the Persian Gulf,* Foreign Affairs, Vol.63, No.1, p.116.

Kennedy, P. (1987) *The Rise and Fall of the Great Powers: Economic Change and Military Conflict from 1500 to 2000.* p.4.

Khuli, F. (1980) *Tribe and State in Bahrain.* University of Chicago Press, Chicago, Illinois, Chapters 5, 6 and 11.

King of Saudi Arabia, (1992) text of speech in: *Al Hayat,* 2 March, p.6.

The Koran: Al Omran Soura, Verse 159. Ash-Shura Soura, Verse 38.

Kung, H. (1986) *Christianity and the World Religions: Paths to Dialogue with Islam, Hinduism, and Buddhism*, Doubleday and Company Inc., Garden City, p.41.

Lawson, F.H. (1989) *Bahrain: The Modernisation of Autocracy*, Westview Press, Boulder, Colorado, Chapter 1-2.

Malik A.B. (1999) *Understanding the Political Behaviour of Islamists: The Implications of Socialisation, Modernisation, and Rationalists Approaches* Studies in Contemporary Islam, Vol.1, No.1, Spring, pp.17-20.

Meadows, P. (1971) *The Many Faces of Change: Exploration in the Theory of Social Change*. Schenkman, Cambridge, Massachusetts.

Nakhleh, E.A. (1990) *"Muntada Al Tanmiyya: Indigenous Scholarship on Development in GCC Countries,"* Paper presented at the Middle East Studies Association Annual Convention, San Antonio, Texas.

Peterson, E.J. (1988) *The Arab Gulf States: Steps Toward Political Participation*, The Washington Papers, No.131, Praeger, New York, pp.84-91.

Peterson, J.E. (1978) *Oman in the Twentieth Century: Political Foundations of an Emerging State*, Croom Helm, London, Chapters 1-2.

Prebish, Raul. 1972 International Economics and Development New York Academic Press.

Qutb, M. (1988) *The Comprehensiveness of Muhammad's Teachings; Private Ownership in Islam*, in: Encyclopaedia of Seerah, Vol.3, Seerah Foundation, London, pp.707-713.

Rahman, A. (1998) *Laws of Inheritance*, in: Encyclopaedia of Seerah, Vol.3, Seerah Foundation, London, pp.733-744.

Rentz, G. (1947) *Muhammad Ibn Abd Al Wahab and the Beginnings of Unitarian Empire in Arabia*, Berkeley, California.

Rostow, W. Whitman. 1960. The Stages of Economic Growth: A non-Communist Manifesto. Cambridge University Press.

Safran, N. (1985) *Saudi Arabia: The Ceaseless Quest for Security*, Harvard University Press, Cambridge, Massachusetts, Chapters 1-2.

Sahih Muslim, Vol.3, Kitab Al-Imara, Hadith No. 4541, pp.102, Obedience to Ruler is Forbidden in Matters Sinful, But is Otherwise Obligatory.

Simons, G. (1998) *Saudi Arabia, the Shape of the Client Feudalism*, Macmillan, pp.196-252.

Wahba, S.H. (1964) *Arabian Days*. Arthur Baker Ltd., London.

Werner, Alt'red. Max Weber. 1975. New York : Abrams

Winder, B. (1965) *Saudi Arabia in the Nineteenth Century*. St. Martin's Press, New York. pp.45-101.

Yapp, M. (1980) *The Nineteenth and Twentieth Centuries* and *British Policy in the Persian Gulf* in: Al Vin J. Cottrell, (ed.), The Persian Gulf States, Johns Hopkins University Press, Baltimore, Massachusetts.

Zahlan, S. R. (1989) *The Creation of Qatar,* Croom Helm, London, Chapters 3-5.

Zaki, A. (1997) *Developmental Changes in Islamic-Arab Movements*, Middle East Affairs Journal,Vol.3, No.1-2, Winter/Spring, pp.3-9.

Zarkally, K. (1985) *The Arabian Peninsula in the days of King Abdul Aziz.* Part 2, Beirut Press, pp.312-431.

Appendices

Appendix I   "Questionnaire"

Appendix II   Articles of the Law of *Majlis Ash-Shura*

Appendix III   Articles of the "Basic Law of Government"

Appendix IV   The Law of the Council of Ministers

Appendix V   The Law of Provinces

Appendix I

QUESTIONNAIRE

Political Development in the Kingdom of Saudi Arabia:
an Assessment of *Majlis Ash-Shura*

A Questionnaire Addressed to Members of the Saudi *Majlis Ash-Shura*

Prepared by
Faisal Ibn Misha'l Al - Su'ud

H.E. Member of *Majlis Ash-Shura*– Saudi Arabia – Riyadh.

Dear Sir,

Thank you for reading this questionnaire and giving me some of your valuable time. This questionnaire is for the purpose of preparing a Ph.D. study in the field of Political Science at the University of Durham, Great Britain. The study is entitled: *Political Development in the Kingdom of Saudi Arabia:* an assessment of Majlis Ash-Shura. The study aims to explore the characteristics and features of the political system and to evaluate its performance, and to evaluate the challenges and developments which confront the system, with particular the establishment of the political institutions thereof. In addition the study will cover the establishment of Majlis Ash-Shura. One of the purposes of this study is to explore the nature of Majlis Ash-Shura, and the mode of its functioning and operation, its activities and achievements. In addition, I aim to identify the points of weakness and strength and ways to develop and enhance its performance and activities.

Your co-operation in answering this questionnaire in due time will have the valuable effect of realizing this study and fulfilling its purposes. The questionnaire will take about fifteen to twenty minutes of your time to complete and your answering of the questions involved will be treated with utmost confidence. We will be pleased to provide you with a copy of this study upon completion. Thank you.

1. Age: _____   Year:_____

2. Place of Birth:

    1. Rural Area   (   )
    2. Village   (   )
    3. Town   (   )

3. Area:

    1. Central Area   (   )
    2. Northern Area   (   )
    3. Southern Area   (   )
    4. Eastern Area   (   )
    5. Western Area   (   )

4. Educational Level:

    1. Holder of Intermediate certificate or less: (   )
    2. Holder of B.Sc.   (   )
    3. Holder of Master's Degree.   (   )
    4. Holder of Ph.D.   (   )

5. Specialization   ……………………………………..

155

6.   Place you received your First Certificate:

       1.   In Saudi Arabia   (   )

       2.   An Arab Country   (   )

       3.   A Western Country   (   )

       4.   Others (please specify)..

7.   What was the position you occupied prior to your membership of Majlis Ash-Shura? ....

8.   Years of practical experience:

       1. Public Sector ....Years.

       2. Private Sector......................Years.

9.   Nature of previous work:

       1.   Administrative.

       2.   Commercial.

       3.   Military.

       4.   Academic.

       5.   Others (please specify)............................

10.   How many years have you spent in Majlis Ash-Shura? ....Years.

11.   In your opinion, what are the most important reasons for establishing Majlis Ash-Shura? (select one or more of the following):

1.   (   )   Expansion of the Kingdom and its functions.
2.   (   )   Completion of state institutions.
3.   (   )   The need to expand political participation.
4.   (   )   To benefit from qualified citizens in realizing the development of the country.
5.   (   )   Demonstration of Ash-Shura efforts in an organized way.
6.   (   )   The need to develop most of the regulations and systems.
7.   (   )   Others (please specify)........................ ....
      ....

12.   What is the extent of your satisfaction with the effective performance by Majlis Ash-Shura of its functions?

1.   Very satisfied   (   )
2.   Satisfied to some extent   (   )
3.   Not sure   (   )
4.   Dissatisfied to some extent   (   )
5.   Very dissatisfied   (   )

13.   How far are you satisfied with the mode or decision-making within Majlis Ash-Shura?

1.   Very satisfied   (   )
2.   Satisfied to some extent   (   )
3.   Not sure   (   )
4.   Dissatisfied to some extent   (   )
5.   Very dissatisfied   (   )

157

14.   What is the extent of the members' freedom to express their viewpoints during Majlis Ash-Shura deliberations?

    1.   Very free   (   )
    2.   Free to some extent.   (   )
    3.   Not sure   (   )
    4.   Limited to some extent (   )
    5.   Very limited   (   )

15.   Are there any consistent groupings, blocs or lobbies within Majlis Ash-Shura which come together prior to the convening of the sessions?

        1.   Yes   (   )
        2.   No   (   )

    Please explain ....

16.   Can any of the members of Majlis Ash-Shura vote against a decision adopted by Majlis Ash-Shura?

        1.   Yes   (   )
        2.   No   (   )

If answer is yes, does that occur?

1. Always   (   )   2. Sometimes   ( ) 3. Seldom ( )

17.   Do you think that voting is conducted with full impartiality?

        1.   Yes   (   )

        2.   No   (   )

If the answer is No, please explain ....

18.   Do all members enjoy equal political weight in voting?

        1.   Yes   (   )

        2.   No   (   )

If the answer is No, please explain ....

19.   Do you think that there is sufficient time to review the issues by members before their being the subject for discussion?

        1.   Yes   (   )

        2.   No.   (   )

If the answer is No, please explain. ....

... ...

20.   Has *Majlis Ash-Shura* ever rejected a bill due to opposition from the majority of members?

        1.   Yes   (   )

        2.   No   (   )

If the answer is Yes, please give examples: ....

....

....

21.   Does a member have the right to consult another member during the
      voting procedure?

                1.   Yes   (   )
                2.   No   (   )

22.   If the answer is Yes, How frequently have you practiced that during
      the current *Majlis Ash-Shura* session before voting was undertaken?

23.   Does a member have the right to abstain from voting?

                1.   Yes   (   )
                2.   No   (   )

24.   If the answer is Yes, Have you ever practiced this right during voting?

                1.   Always   (   )
                2.   Sometimes   (   )
                3.   Seldom   (   )

25. Do you receive any requests from the surrounding community to study particular issues?

       1.   Always   (   )

       2.   Sometimes   (   )

       3.   Seldom   (   )

26. Is there any pressure exerted upon you by the government so as to pass a particular bill?

       1.   Always   (   )

       2.   Sometimes   (   )

       3.   Seldom   (   )

       4.   No.   (   ).

27. Does the government refer to *Majlis Ash-Shura* in taking particularly important decisions?

       1.   Always   (   )

       2.   Sometimes   (   )

       3.   Seldom   (   )

28. Does *Majlis Ash-Shura* have the authority to reject bills because it is acting outside its specialization or for any other reason?

       1.   Yes   (   )

       2.   No   (   )

29.   To what extent do you see Majlis Ash-Shura as useful in rationalizing
       political decisions?

       1.   Very useful   (   )
       2.   Useful to some extent   (   )
       3.   Not sure   (   )
       4.   Not useful to some extent   (   )
       5.   Absolutely not useful   (   )

30.   What is the effect of Majlis Ash-Shura delegations upon the process
       of decision undertaken by the government?

31.   What is the most suitable number for the membership of Majlis Ash-
       Shura, according to your own viewpoint?

       1.   60 members   (   )
       2.   90 members   (   )
       3.   More than 90   (   )

32.   If you suggest increasing or decreasing the current membership of
       Majlis Ash-Shura, please put your personal justifications for doing so:

. . . .

. . . .

. . . .

33.   Had any member or group of members of Majlis Ash-Shura ever suggested a bill to be studied by Majlis Ash-Shura?

        1.   Always   (   )

        2.   Sometimes   (   )

        3.   Seldom   (   )

34.   What do you think is the most suitable method for selecting the members of Majlis Ash-Shura?

1. Appointment method   (   )

2. Voting method   (   )

3. A mixture of appointment / voting method   (   )

4. Any other method you suggest (please specify):   (   )

Why have you selected this method in particular?

. . . .

. . . .

35.   Do you expect that there might be any development in the method of selecting the membership of *Majlis Ash-Shura* in the future?

1.   Yes   (   )   2.   No   (   ).

36.   What is the extent of awareness of citizens' concerning the effectiveness of Majlis Ash-Shura according to your own thinking?

1.   Very high   (   )
2.   High to some extent   (   )
3.   Not sure   (   )
4.   Low to some extent   (   )
5.   Very Low   (   ).

37.   If you consider that citizens' awareness of the effectiveness of Majlis Ash-Shura is very low, what are the reasons for that in your viewpoint? And what are the solutions thereto?

. . . .

. . . .

. . . .

38.   Do you see Majlis Ash-Shura as the body representing all categories of the community?

1.Yes   (   )   2. To some extent (   )
3. No   (   )

164

39. What are the most important prerequisites to be reflected by Majlis Ash-Shura membership?

1. . . . .

2. . . . .

3. . . . .

40. What are the basis and standards to be taken into consideration while selecting Majlis Ash-Shura members?

1.	Geographical and Regional.	(	)
2.	Tribal and Social.	(	)
3.	Educational (specialization and experience)	(	)
4.	Other bases and standards (please specify)	(	)

41. On which of Majlis Ash-Shura committees do you serve?

1. Islamic Affairs Committee.

2. Foreign Affairs Committee.

3. Security Affairs Committee.

4. Economic and Financial Affairs Committee.

5. Social and Health Affairs Committee.

6. Educational, Cultural and Information Affairs Committee.

7. Services and Public Facilities' Affairs Committee.

8. Regulations and Administration Affairs Committee.

9. Another Committee (please specify) . . . .

165

42. Is the nature of the committee in which you work in harmony with your specialization?

    1.   Yes   (   )   2.   No.   (   )

43. Do you want to continue in the membership of this committee?

    1.   Yes   (   )   2.   No.   (   )

    If the answer is No. please specify: . . . .

    . . . .

44. Do you think that the committee includes suitable personnel to carry its missions and responsibilities?

    1.   Yes   (   )   2.   No.   (   )

    If the answer is No, please specify the categories that you suggest should be included? . . . .
    . . . .

45. When does the committee convene?

    1. Weekly   (   )   2. Every couple of Weeks ( ).
    3. Every couple of Months (   )   4. On request   ( ).
    5. Every month (   )   6. Others (specify). . . . .
        . . . .
        . . . .

166

46.   Are some of the members absent from the meetings?

1. Always   (   )   2. Sometimes   (   )   3. Seldom (   )

47.   How is the programme of Majlis Ash-Shura Sessions prepared?

. . . .
. . . .
. . . .

48.   Does it discuss issues that are not already listed in Majlis Ash-Shura agenda?

1. Yes (   )   2. No   (   ) 3.   Seldom   (   )

49.   Does *Majlis Ash-Shura* convene at times of crisis?

1. Yes (   )   2. No   (   ) 3. Seldom   (   )

50.   What is your general viewpoint concerning the participation of committee members?

1.   Most of the member's participation is just a formality.

2.   Most of the member's participation is real and effective.

3.   It depends upon the nature of the issue in question.

167

51.   How does Majlis Ash-Shura normally deal with the recommendations of the specialized committees?

    1.   It adopts its recommendations without any amendments.
    2.   It adopts its recommendations with some amendments.
    3.   It refers items back to the Commission for further studying.

52.   What is the degree of effectiveness of the committee in which you work regarding the performance of its missions and responsibilities?

    1.   Very high   (   )
    2.   High to some extent   (   )
    3.   Not sure   (   )
    4.   Low to some extent   (   )
    5.   Very Low   (   )

53.   If the effectiveness of the committee is very low, specify the reasons from your own viewpoint?

    . . . .
    . . . .
    . . . .

54.   Do you think that there is a need to establish a new committee?

    1. Yes   (   )   2. No.   (   )

55.   If the answer is Yes, what is the committee that you suggest and what
        are its outstanding criteria?

        . . . .

        . . . .

56.   What is the difference between the Saudi Majlis Ash-Shura of
        Consultation and that of other Parliaments available in other Arab
        and Gulf countries (Qatar, Oman and Bahrain) according to your own
        viewpoint?

        . . . .

        . . . .

        . . . .

57.   What is the difference between the Saudi Majlis Ash-Shura and the
        parliaments of Western countries, according to your own viewpoint?

        . . . .

        . . . .

        . . . .

58.   What are the outstanding difficulties that face you while you are
        working at Majlis Ash-Shura?

        1. . . . .

        2. . . . .

169

3. . . . .

59.   What are your suggestions for overcoming these difficulties?

1. . . . .

2. . . . .

3. . . . .

60.   What do you think are the most outstanding positive points and
strengths that Majlis Ash-Shura is enjoying according to your own
point of view?

. . . .

. . . .

. . . .

. . . .

61.   What do you think are the most outstanding negative points and
weaknesses that Majlis Ash-Shura is suffering from, according to
your own point of view?

. . . .

. . . .

. . . .

62.   What are your viewpoints and suggestions for enhancing and developing the performance and effectiveness of the Saudi Majlis Ash-Shura?

. . . .

. . . .

. . . .

. . . .

THANK YOU VERY MUCH

Appendix II

THE LAW OF MAJLIS ASH-SHURA

Article 1

In compliance with the words of Almighty Allah:

> "It is part of the mercy of *Allah* that thou dealest gently with them. Were thou not serve and hadst thou not hardened thy heart, they would have broken away from about thee, so pass over (their faults) and ask for (*Allah's*) forgiveness for them, and consult them in affairs (*of moment*) then, when thou has taken a decision, put thy trust in Allah. For Allah loveth those who put their trust in him."

Source (CXI, 159)
and his other word:

> "Those who respond to their lord and establish regular prayer who (conduct) their affairs by mutual consultation, who spend out of what we bestow on them for sustenance..."

Source (XL 38);
and following Al Sunna of his Messenger who consulted his companions and urged the nation to engage in consultation, Majlis Ash-Shura shall be established to exercise all tasks entrusted to it according to this law and the basic law of government while adhering to the Book of Allah and Al Sunna of the Messenger maintaining brotherly ties and co-operating in kindness and piety.

Article 2

Majlis Ash-Shura shall hold fast to the rope of Allah and pledge itself to the sources of Islamic legislation. All members of Majlis Ash-Shura shall ever serve in the public interest and shall preserve the unity of the community, the entity of the state and the interest of the nation.

Article 3

Majlis Ash-Shura shall consist of a chairman and ninety members chosen by the King from among the scholars and men of knowledge, expertise and specialisation. Their duties and all other affairs shall be defined by a royal order.

Article 4

It is stipulated that every member of Majlis Ash-Shura shall be:

One.   a Saudi national by birth and descent,

Two.   a competent person of recognised good character, and

Three.   not younger than 30 years of age.

Article 5

Any member may submit a request to resign his membership to the Chairman of Majlis Ash-Shura, who in turn shall refer it to the king.

Article 6

If a member of Majlis Ash-Shura neglects the duties of his work he shall be investigated and tried according to rules and measures to be issued by royal order.

Article 7

If a member's place in Majlis Ash-Shura becomes vacant for any reason, the King shall choose a replacement and issue a royal order to this effect.

Article 8

No member of Majlis Ash-Shura shall exploit his membership in his own interest.

Article 9

Membership of Majlis Ash-Shura shall not be combined with any governmental post, or with the management of any company, unless the King deems it necessary.

Article 10

The Chairman, his Deputy and the Secretary General of Majlis Ash-Shura shall be appointed and relieved by royal orders. Their salaries, duties and all their other affairs shall be defined by a royal order.

Article 11

Prior to assumption of their duties, the Chairman, the Members and the Secretary General of Majlis Ash-Shura shall take the following oath before the king:

"I swear by Almighty Allah to be loyal to my religion, then to my king and country I swear not to reveal any of the secrets of state, to protect its interests and laws and to perform my duties with sincerity, integrity, loyalty and fairness".

174

Article 12

The city of Riyadh is the seat of Majlis Ash-Shura. Majlis Ash-Shura may convene in another area within the Kingdom if the King deems it necessary.

Article 13

The fixed term of Majlis Ash-Shura shall be four years, effective from the date of the royal order issued for the formation of Majlis. A new Majlis shall be formed at least two months before the end of the current Majlis term. If the term expires before the formation of the new Majlis, the previous one shall remain active until a new Majlis is formed. When a new Majlis be formed, the number of the newly selected members shall not be less than 50% of the entire Majlis' members.

Article 14

The king, or whomever he may deputise, shall deliver an annual royal speech at Majlis Ash-Shura on the domestic and foreign policy of the State.

Article 15

Majlis Ash-Shura shall express its opinion on the general policies of the state referred by the Prime Minister, specifically, Majlis shall have the right to do the following:

One.   Discuss the general plan for economic and social development.
Two.   Study laws and by-laws, international treaties and agreements, and concessions, and make whatever suggestion it deems appropriate.
Three.   Interpret laws.
Four.   Discuss annual reports forwarded by ministries and other governmental institutions, and make whatever suggestions it deems appropriate.

Article 16

No meeting held by Majlis Ash-Shura shall be considered official without a quorum of at least two-thirds of its members, including the chairman or his deputy. Resolutions shall not be considered official without majority approval.

Article 17

The resolutions of Majlis Ash-Shura shall be forwarded to the Prime Minister. If the views of both councils are in agreement, the resolutions shall come into force following the king's approval. If the views are in disagreement, the king may decide what he deems appropriate.

Article 18
Laws, international treaties and agreements, and concessions shall be issued and amended by royal decrees after being studied by Majlis Ash-Shura.

Article 19
Majlis Ash-Shura shall form specialised committees from amongst its members to exercise the powers within its jurisdiction. Majlis may also form other specialised committees to discuss any items on the agenda.

Article 20
Majlis Ash-Shura's committees may seek the help of others who are not members of Majlis, with the chairman's approval.

Article 21
Majlis Ash-Shura shall have a general commission composed of the chairman, his deputy and the heads of the specialised committees.

Article 22
The Chairman of Majlis Ash-Shura shall submit requests to the Chairman of the Council of Ministers. To summon any government official to the meeting of Majlis Ash-Shura when matters relating to his jurisdiction are discussed. The official shall have the right to debate but not the right to vote.

Article 23
Any group of ten members of Majlis Ash-Shura have the right to propose a new draft law or an amendment to a law already in force and submit it to the chairman of Majlis. The Chairman shall submit the proposal to the king.

Article 24
The chairman of Majlis Ash-Shura shall submit a request to the Prime Minister to provide Majlis with information and documents in the processions of government institutions, which Majlis believes are necessary to facilitate its work.

Article 25
The chairman of Majlis Ash-Shura shall submit an annual report to the king on its work in accordance with Majlis' by-law.

Article 26
Civil service laws shall apply to employees of the secretariat of Majlis unless its by-laws stipulate to the contrary.

Article 27
Majlis Ash-Shura shall be allocated a special budget to be approved by the king. It shall be spent in accordance with rules to be issued by royal order.

Article 28
Majlis Ash-Shura's financial matters and the auditing and closing of accounts shall be carried out in accordance with special rules to be issued by royal order.

Article 29
The by-laws of Majlis Ash-Shura shall define the functions of the Chairman of Majlis Ash-Shura, his Deputy, the Secretary General of Majlis, the Secretariat, the methods of conducting its sessions, the management of its work and its committees' work and the voting procedure. The regulations shall also specify rules of debate, the forms of response and other procedures conducive to restraint and discipline within Majlis. It shall exercise its powers for the good of the Kingdom and the prosperity of its people. These regulations shall be issued by royal order.

Article 30
This law can be amended only in the same manner in which it was promulgated.

THE BY-LAWS OF MAJLIS ASH-SHURA

Jurisdiction of the Chairman of Majlis, His Deputy and the Secretary General

Article 1
The chairman of Majlis shall supervise all functions of Majlis, shall represent it at other agencies and organisations and shall be its spokesman.

Article 2
The chairman of Majlis shall head all sessions of Majlis and the steering committee as well as any committee meetings he attends.

Article 3

The chairman of Majlis Ash-Shura shall open and close Majlis sessions, chair meetings, moderate and participate in deliberations, give the floor to speakers, specify the topic for discussion, draw the attention of speakers to the time limit and the subject matter of discussion, end discussions and move motions. He may do whatever he deems necessary to maintain order during sessions.

Article 4

The chairman of Majlis Ash-Shura may call Majlis, the Steering Committee or any other committee for an emergency meeting to discuss a specific topic.

Article 5

The Deputy Chairman of Majlis Ash-Shura shall assist the chairman in his presence and assume his duties in his absence.

Article 6

The Deputy Chairman shall preside over Majlis and Steering Committee sessions when the chairman is absent, and in case both are absent whomsoever is designated by the king shall preside over Majlis. The Deputy Chairman and the king's designee shall have the same jurisdiction as those specified for the Chairman.

Article 7

The Secretary General or whosoever represents him shall attend Majlis and Steering Committee sessions. He shall supervise the taking of the minutes and announce the schedule and the agenda of the sessions. In addition he shall attend to all duties assigned by Majlis, by the Steering Committee or by the Chairman of Majlis. He shall answer to the Chairman of Majlis for all the financial and administrative affairs to Majlis.

The Steering Committee of Majlis

Article 8

The Steering Committee shall consist of Chairman of Majlis, his deputy and heads of specialised committees.

Article 9

A Steering Committee meeting shall not be official unless attended by at least two-thirds of the members. It shall pass resolutions by majority vote. In case of a tie, the chairman shall cast the deciding vote.

Article 10

The minutes of every meeting of the steering committee shall indicate the time and place of the meeting, the names of those present, the names of those absent, a synopsis of the deliberations and the full text of the recommendations. The minutes shall be signed by the Chairman of Majlis and attending members.

Article 11

The Steering Committee shall have authority over the following:

a. The preparation of a general plan for Majlis and its committees to enable it to realize its objectives.
b. The preparation of an agenda for Majlis meetings.
c. The reaching of final decisions regarding objections to the minutes of a session, the result of pooling, the counting of votes or any other objections raised sessions and its decision during in this regard shall be final.
e. The making of rules of procedure for Majlis and its committees in accordance with the rules and regulations of Majlis.

Session

Article 12

Majlis Ash-Shura shall hold one ordinary session at least once a fortnight. The date and time of a session shall be decided by the Chairman. The Chairman may advance or postpone sessions when necessary.

Article 13

The agenda of a session shall be distributed to all members ahead of time along with reports pertaining to agenda items and whatever else the Steering Committee of Majlis deems necessary.

Article 14

A member of Majlis Ash-Shura must study the items on the agenda on the premises of Majlis, and he shall never, under any circumstances, take any papers, draft laws or documents related to his work outside the premises of Majlis.

Article 15

A member shall submit in writing a request to address Majlis during sessions, and requests shall be honoured in order of receipt.

Article 16
The Chairman shall allow a member to speak taking into consideration the order of receipt of his request and the public interest.

Article 17
A member shall not speak on a single topic for more than ten minutes, unless allowed otherwise by the Chairman. A member shall only address the chairman of Majlis, and none but the chairman shall be allowed to interrupt the member.

Article 18
Majlis may postpone or restudy a certain topic and the chairman may temporarily adjourn for no more than one hour.

Article 19
Each session shall be recorded in minutes which state the venue and date of the session, the time it started, the name of the chairman, the number of members present, the names of those absent, and the reasons for their absences, if any, a summary of discussions, the numbers of those voting in favour and those voting against, the result of the voting, the texts of resolutions, all that is related to the postponement or suspension of the session and the time of its adjournment, as well as any other matters the chairman deems necessary.

Article 20
The chairman of Majlis as well as the Secretary General or his deputy shall sign the minutes after they are read to the members and any member has the right to study them if he wishes.

Committees

Article 21
Majlis Ash-Shura shall, at the outset of each term, form the necessary specialised committees from among Majlis members to exercise its jurisdiction.

Article 22
Each specialised committee shall be formed of a number of members to be determined by Majlis, provided the number is not less than five. Majlis shall also name these members, the committee chairman and his deputy, taking into consideration members, qualifications and committee needs. Majlis shall also form ad hoc committees to study certain issues and each of the specialised committees can form sub-committees from among its members to study specific issues.

180

Article 23
Majlis may reconstitute its specialised committees and form new ones.

Article 24
A committee chairman shall manage the work of the committee and speak on its behalf before Majlis. When the chairman is absent, his deputy shall take over. The most senior committee member chairs the committee when the chairman and his deputy are absent.

Article 25
A committee meets upon the call of the committee chairman, Majlis or the Chairman of Majlis.

Article 26
Committee meetings shall be held in camera, and they shall not be considered legal unless a minimum of two-thirds of the committee members are present. Each committee shall write down its agenda upon its chairman request, and shall issue its recommendation by the majority of the members present. The chairman shall cast the deciding vote when votes are equal.

Article 27
A committee shall study whatever issues are referred to them by Majlis or the Chairman of Majlis, and if the issue concerns more than one committee, the Chairman shall decide which committee studies the issue first or may refer it to a joint committee of all the members of the committee concerned under the chairmanship of the Chairman of Majlis or his Deputy.

Article 28
Any Majlis member may express his opinion on any issue that has been referred to one of the specialised committees, even if he is not a member of that committee, provided that he presents his opinion in writing to the Chairman of Majlis.

Article 29
Minutes shall be taken of each committee meeting, stating the date and venue of the meeting, the names of members present and absent, a summary of the discussions and the text of its recommendations. The Chairman and the members present shall sign the minutes.

Article 30

When study of a certain issue is complete, a committee shall write a report that explains the issue, the committee's point of view, its recommendations and their bases. If there is a minority point of view it shall also be included.

Voting and the Adoption of Resolutions

Article 31

Majlis resolutions shall be adopted by majority as provided by article 16 of the Law of Majlis Ash-Shura. In case a majority is not achieved the issue shall be scheduled for voting in the next session, in the event of the issue not winning a majority in the second session, the issue shall be referred to the king along with what ever studies have been completed concerning it, as well as the results of voting in both sessions.

Article 32

No deliberations nor presentations of new opinions shall be allowed during the voting process. In all cases, the chairman should cast his vote after all the members have voted.

General Provisions

Article 33

The chairman of Majlis Ash-Shura shall submit his annual report as provided in Article 25 of the Law of Majlis within the first three months of the new year. This report shall include all the studies and projects carried out in the previous year in addition to all resolutions passed and the current status of all pending issues.

Article 34

The financial and personnel affairs of Majlis shall be managed in accordance with the by-laws regulating Majlis' financial and personnel affairs.

The Chairman of Majlis shall issue the rules necessary for regulating the financial and administrative functions of Majlis, including the organisation hierarchy and the tasks of the various offices of Majlis, in accordance with the law of Majlis and its by-laws.

BY-LAWS ON THE RIGHTS AND DUTIES
of Members of Majlis Ash-Shura

Article 1
Membership in Majlis Ash-Shura shall take effect from the beginning of Majlis' term as specified in the order for its formation according to Article 13 of the Law of Majlis. A substitute members' term of office shall commence on the date specified in the royal order nominating him and shall expire at the end of Majlis' term. In case the term of Majlis should end before the new Majlis is formed, his membership shall remain valid until the new Majlis is formed, unless his membership is terminated.

Article 2
The member of Majlis Ash-Shura shall receive a monthly remuneration of SR 20,000 during his term of office and shall be treated like a 15th grade employee as far as allowances, compensations, privileges and increments are concerned. All this shall not affect the pension that a member may deserve.

Article 3
A full time Majlis member shall retain the position and grade he held before joining Majlis. His term of office in Majlis shall be taken into consideration with respect to merit increases, promotions and retirement. A member shall pay, during membership, his pension premiums according to his basic salary.

A member shall not receive both Majlis remuneration and the salary from his other position at the same time.

In case a member's salary exceeds his remuneration in Majlis, Majlis shall pay the member the difference. If the members' position provides him with greater benefits than those provided by Majlis, the member shall continue to receive them.

Article 4
As an exception to Article 2 of these By-laws, the forty-five day period that coincides with the 1st day of Leo to the end of the 14th day of Virgo will be

the members' annual leave. If during this leave any urgent matter arises and it requires the jurisdiction of Majlis Ash-Shura, then the Council of Ministers will act on it according to its bylaws and shall refer the matter and decision to Majlis Ash-Shura to seek the opinion of its members after the end of their leave.

Amendment by Royal Order A/97 dated 17-2-1418

Article 5
A member should be impartial and objective in all his functions at Majlis. He shall not raise before Majlis private or personal issues nor any issue contrary to the public interest.

Article 6
A member shall attend sessions and committee meetings regularly. He shall also notify the Chairman of Majlis or a committee chairman in writing the event if he is not being able to attend a Majlis session or a committee meeting. Moreover, he shall not leave a session nor a meeting before adjournment without permission from the Chairman.

Financial and Personnel Affairs

Article 1
Majlis fiscal year is the same as that of the state.

Article 2
Majlis Ash-Shura shall prepare a draft of Majlis annual budget and forward it to the king for approval.

Article 3
Majlis budget shall be deposited with the Arab Monetary Agency and withdrawal therefrom shall be against the signature of the Chairman or his Deputy.

Article 4
In case Majlis' budget does not cover all Majlis expenditure, or an unforeseen expense arises, the Chairman shall forward a memorandum for the required additional funds to the king for approval.

Article 5
Remuneration for titles and grades of positions at Majlis shall be determined in the budget and may be modified during the fiscal year by a decision of the Chairman.

Article 6
14th and 15th grade positions shall be filled by royal consent while other positions shall be filled according to law and by-laws of the Civil Service with exemption from competition.

Article 7
The steering committee of Majlis shall set rules for the remuneration of non-members who render Majlis service, be they government officials or others. As far as remuneration is concerned these rules shall be issued by a decision from the Chairman of Majlis.

Article 8
Majlis Ash-Shura shall not be audited by any other body and within the administrative structure of Majlis, where there shall be an accounting department. The Steering Committee of Majlis shall undertake the auditing. The Chairman may assign a financial or administrative expert to write a report on any of Majlis' financial or administrative affairs.

Article 9
At the end of the fiscal year, the General Secretariat shall prepare the final statement of accounts, and the chairman of Majlis shall forward it to the king for approval.

Article 10
Without contravention of these By-laws, Majlis shall follow the rules pertaining to the accounts of ministers and government agencies to regulate Majlis' financial affairs.

Rules and Procedures for Investigation and the Trial
of Majlis Ash-Shura Members

Article 1

If a member of Majlis Ash-Shura neglects any of the duties of his work, one of the following actions shall be taken against him:

a.   A written reprimand shall be directed to him.
b.   He shall be fined one month's salary.
c.   His membership shall be terminated

Article 2

A committee of three Majlis members selected by Majlis Chairman shall conduct the investigation.

Article 3

The committee shall inform the member concerned of the alleged misconduct. The committee shall also record his rebuttal in the proceedings of the investigation. The committee shall then report its verdict to the Steering Committee of Majlis.

Article 4

The Steering Committee may also form a three-member committee, excluding the Chairman and his Deputy, to investigate the alleged misconduct of the given member. This committee shall be entitled to apply the penalty or a written reprimand or a fine of one month's salary.

If the committee concludes that the member should be expelled, the verdict shall be referred to Majlis Chairman, who shall in turn, refer it to the king.

Article 5

The application of any of the above penalties does not preclude the initiation of public or private claims against the member.

Appendix III

The Basic Government Law

The Custodian of the Two Holy Mosques, King Fahd Bin Abd - al Aziz Al - Su'ud issued a Royal Decree embodying the Basic Government Law. The following is the text of the Decree.

In the name of God, the Most Compassionate, the Most Merciful,

N: A/90
Dated : 27th Shaban 1412H

With the help of God, we, Fahd bin Abd - al Aziz Al-Su'ud, Monarch of the Kingdom of Saudi Arabia, having taken into consideration the public interest, and in view of the progress of the State in various fields and out of the desire to achieve the objectives we are pursuing, having decreed the following:

1. The promulgation of the Basic Law of Government as the attached text,
2. That all regulations, orders and decrees in force shall remain valid when this Basic Law comes into force, until they are amended to conform with it,
3. That this decree shall be published in the official Gazette, and shall come into force on the date of its publication.

In the name of God, the Most Compassionate the Most Merciful,

The Basic Law of Government

Chapter One

General Principles

Article 1
The Kingdom of Saudi Arabia is a sovereign Arab Islamic State. Its religion is Islam. Its constitution is Almighty God's Book, The Holy *Kurān*, and Al Sunna (Tradition) of the Prophet (Pbuh). Arabic is the language of the Kingdom. The City of Riyadh is the capital.

Article 2
The State's public holidays are Eid Al Fitr (the Feast of Ramadan) and Eid Al Adha (The Feast of the Sacrifice). Its calendar follows the Hijri year (the lunar year).

Article 3
The flag of the State is as follows:

One.   Its colour is green.

Two.   Its width equals two thirds of its length.

Three.   The words, "There is no god but God and Mohammed is His Messenger" are inscribed in the centre, with a drawn sword underneath. The flag should never be inverted.

The Law will specify the rules pertaining to the flag.

Article 4
The State's emblem represents two crossed swords with a palm tree in the middle of the upper space between them. The law will define the State's anthem and medals.

Chapter Two

The Law of Government

Article 5

One.   Monarchy is the system of rule in the Kingdom of Saudi Arabia.

Two.   The rulers of the country shall be taken from amongst the sons of the founder King Abd - al Aziz Bin Abd - al Rahman Al Faisal Al - Su'ud, and their descendants. The most upright among them shall receive allegiance according to Almighty God's Book and His Messenger's Sunna (The Tradition).

Three.   The King shall choose the Crown Prince and relieve him of his duties by a Royal Decree.

Four.   The Crown Prince shall devote himself exclusively to his duties as Crown Prince and shall perform any other duties delegated to him by the King.

Five.   Upon the death of the King, the Crown Prince shall assume the Royal powers until a pledge of allegiance (bay'a) is given.

Article 6

In support of the Book of God and Al Sunna of His Messenger, citizens shall give the pledge of allegiance (bay`a) to the King, professing loyalty in times of hardship and ease.

Article 7

Government in the Kingdom of Saudi Arabia derives its authority from the Book of God and Al Sunna of the Prophet, which are the ultimate sources of reference for this Law and the other laws of the State.

Article 8

Government in the Kingdom of Saudi Arabia is based on justice, shura (consultation) and equality according to Islamic Shari`a.

Chapter Three

The Values of Saudi Society

Article 9

The family is the nucleus of Saudi Society. Members of the family shall be raised in the Islamic creed, which demands allegiance and obedience to God, to His Prophet and to the rulers, respect for and obedience to the laws and love for and pride in the homeland and its glorious history.

Article 10

The state shall aspire to promote family bonds and Arab-Islamic values. It shall take care of all individuals and provide the right conditions for the growth of their talents and skills.

Article 11

Saudi Society is based on full adherence to God's guidance. Members of this society shall co-operate amongst themselves in charity, piety and cohesion.

Article 12

Consolidation of the national unity is a duty. The State shall forbid all activities that may lead to division, disorder and partition.

Article 13
The aim of education is to implant the Islamic creed in the hearts of all youths, to help them acquire knowledge and skills, to qualify them to become useful members of their society, to love their homeland and take pride in its history.

Chapter Four

Economic Principles

Article 14
All natural resources that God has deposited underground, above ground, in territorial waters or within the land and sea domains under the authority of the state, together with revenues of these resources, shall be the property of the state, as provided by the law.

The law shall specify means for exploitation, protection and development of these resources in the best interest of the state and its security and economy.

Article 15
No concessions or licenses to exploit any public resources of the country shall be granted unless authorised by provisions of the law.

Article 16
Public funds are inviolable. They shall be protected by the state and safeguarded by all citizens and residents.

Article 17
Ownership, capital and labour are basic components of the economic and social entity of the Kingdom. They are personal rights which perform a social function in accordance with the Islamic Shari`a.

Article 18
The State shall guarantee private ownership and its sanctity. No one shall be deprived of his private property, unless in service of the public interest. In this case, fair compensation shall be given to him.

Article 19
General confiscation of assets is prohibited. No confiscation of an individual's assets shall be enforced without a judicial ruling.

Article 20
No taxes or fees shall be imposed, except in need and on a just basis. Imposition, amendment, cancellation or exemption shall take place according to the provisions of the law.

Article 21
Zakat shall be collected and spent for legitimate expenses.

Article 22
Economic and social development shall be carried out according to a fair, wise plan.

Chapter Five

Rights and Duties

Article 23
The State shall protect the Islamic creed, apply the Shari'a, encourage good and discourage evil and undertake its duty regarding the Propagation of Islam (Da'wa).

Article 24
The State shall develop and maintain the two holy mosques. It shall provide care and security to pilgrims to help them perform their Hajj and Umra and visit the Prophet's mosque in ease and comfort.

Article 25
The State will nourish the aspirations of Arab and Muslim nations in solidarity and harmony and strengthen relations with friendly states.

Article 26
The State shall protect human rights in accordance with the Shari`a.

Article 27
The State shall guarantee the rights of the citizens and their families in cases of emergency, illness, disability and old age. The State shall support the Social Insurance Law and encourage organisations and individuals to participate in philanthropic activities.

Article 28
The State shall facilitate job opportunities for every able person, and enact laws to protect the worker and the employer.

Article 29
The State shall patronise sciences, letters and culture. It shall encourage scientific research, protect the Islamic and Arab heritage and contribute towards Arab, Islamic and human civilisation.

Article 30
The state shall provide public education and commit itself to the eradication of illiteracy.

Article 31
The state shall look after public health and provide health care for every citizen.

Article 32
The state shall work towards the preservation, protection and improvement of the environment as well as preventing pollution.

Article 33
The state shall form armed forces and equip them to defend the Islamic creed, the two holy mosques, the society and the homeland.

Article 34
It shall be the duty of every citizen to defend the Islamic creed, the society and homeland. The law shall specify rules for military service.

Article 35
The law shall specify rules pertaining to Saudi Arabian nationality.

Article 36

The State shall provide security for all citizens and residents on its territories. No one may be confined, arrested or imprisoned without reference to the law.

Article 37

Dwellings are inviolate. Access is prohibited without their owners' permission. No search may be made except in cases specified by the law.

Article 38

No one shall be punished for another's crimes. No conviction or penalty shall be inflicted without reference to the Shari'a or the provisions of the law. Punishment shall not be imposed *ex post facto*.

Article 39

The mass media and all other vehicles of expression shall employ civil and polite language, contribute towards the education of the nation and strengthen unity. It is prohibited to commit acts leading to disorder and division, affecting the security of the state and its public relations, or undermining human dignity and rights. Details shall be specified in the law.

Article 40

The privacy of telegraphic and postal communications, telephone and other means of communication shall be inviolate. There shall be no confiscation, delay surveillance or eavesdropping, except in cases provided by the law.

Article 41

Residents in the Kingdom of Saudi Arabia shall abide by its laws, observe the values of the Saudi community and respect Saudi traditions and feelings.

Article 42

The state shall grant the right of political asylum provided it is in the public interest. International agreements and laws shall define rules and procedures for the extradition of common criminals.

Article 43

Councils held by the King and the Crown Prince shall be open for all citizens and anyone else who may have a complaint or a grievance. A citizen shall be entitled to address public authorities and discuss any matters of concern to him.

Chapter Six

The Authorities of the State

Article 44
The Authorities of the State consist of:
- The Judicial Authority.
- The Executive Authority
- The Regulatory Authority.

These authorities will co-operate in the performance of their functions, according to this Law or other laws. The King is the ultimate arbiter for these authorities.

Article 45
The Holy Kurān and Al Sunna (Tradition) of God's Messenger shall be the source for fatwas (religious advisory rulings). The Law shall specify hierarchical organisation for the composition of the Council of the Senior U'lema, the Research Administration and the Office of the Mufti, together with their functions.

Article 46
The Judiciary is an independent authority. The decisions of judges shall not be subject to any authority other than the authority of the Islamic Shari'a.

Article 47
All people, either citizens or residents in the Kingdom, are entitled to file suits on an equal basis. The law shall specify procedures for this purpose.

Article 48
The courts shall apply rules of the Islamic Shari'a in cases that are brought before them, according to the Holy Kurān and Al Sunna, and according to laws which are decreed by the ruler in agreement with the Holy Kurān and Al Sunna.

Article 49
The Courts are empowered to arbitrate in all disputes and crimes, taking into account the provision of Article 53 of this law.

Article 50
The King or whomsoever he may deputise shall concern himself with the implementation of judicial rulings.

Article 51
The law shall specify the composition of the Supreme Judiciary Council and its functions, as well as the hierarchy for the courts and their functions.

Article 52
Judges shall be appointed and relieved by Royal Decree, based on a proposal of the Supreme Judiciary Council, in accordance with provisions of the law.

Article 53
The law shall specify the hierarchy of the Board of Grievances and its functions.

Article 54
The law shall specify the relationship between the Commission of Inquiry and the Attorney General and their organisation and functions.

Article 55
The King shall rule the nation according to the Shari'a. He shall also supervise the implementation of the Shari'a, the general policy of the State and the defence and protection of the country.

Article 56
The King is the Prime Minister. Members of the Council of Ministers shall assist him in the performance of his mission according to the provisions of this law and other laws. The Council of Ministers law shall specify the powers of the Council in respect of internal and external affairs, organisation of governmental departments and their co-ordination. In addition, the law shall specify the qualifications and the powers of the ministers, ministerial accountability procedures and all matters pertaining to the ministers. The law of the Council of Ministers and the areas of their authority may be amended according to this law.

Article 57
a.   The King shall appoint and relieve deputies of the Prime Minister and member ministers of the Council by Royal Decree.
b.   Deputies of the Prime Minister and member ministers of the Council shall be jointly

---

195

responsible to the King for the implementation of the Shari'a, laws and the general policy of the State.

c.　　The King is entitled to dissolve and reconstitute the Council of Ministers.

Article 58
The King shall appoint those who are at the rank of ministers and deputy ministers, and those who are at the highest grade and relieve them by a Royal Decree as provided by the Law. Ministers and head of independent departments shall be answerable to the King in respect of the ministers and agencies they head.

Article 59
The law shall specify the rules of the Civil Service, including salaries, awards, compensations, privileges and pensions.

Article 60
The King is the Supreme Commander of the Armed Forces. He shall appoint and dismiss officers from service, as provided by terms of the law.

Article 61
The King shall announce any state or emergency or general mobilisation and shall declare war. The law shall specify rules for this purpose.

Article 62
If an imminent danger is threatening the safety of the Kingdom, the integrity of its territories or the security and interests of its people, or is impeding the functions of official organisations, the King may take urgent measures to deal with such a danger. When he considers that these measures should continue, necessary arrangements shall be made in accordance with the law.

Article 63
The king shall receive kings and heads of states, appoint his representatives to other states and receive credentials of other states' representatives accredited to him.

Article 64
The king shall award medals according to provisions of the law.

Article 65
The king may delegate some powers of authority to the Crown Prince by royal decree.

Article 66
Should the king happen to travel abroad, he shall issue a royal decree to deputise the crown prince to manage the affairs of State and look after the interests of the people, as set out in the royal decree.

Article 67
The Regulatory Authority shall be concerned with the making of laws and regulations which will safeguard all interests, and remove evil from the state's affairs, according to Shari'a. Its powers shall be exercised according to provisions of this law and the law of the Council of Ministers and the Law of the Shura Council.

Article 68
The Shura Council shall be established. Its law shall specify the details of its formation, powers and selection of members. The King may dissolve and reconstitute Majlis Ash Shura.

Article 69
The King may summon Majlis Ash Shura and the Council of Ministers for a joint session. He may summon others whom he deems necessary to attend the meeting and discuss whatever affairs he considers fit.

Article 70
Laws, international agreements, treaties and concessions shall be approved and amended by royal decrees.

Article 71
Laws shall be published in the Official Gazette, and implemented effective from the date of publication, unless another date is specified.

Chapter Seven

Financial Affairs

Article 72
a.   The Law shall include provisions for the State's revenues and their depositing with the General Treasury of the State.

b.   Revenues shall be recorded and spent according to procedures stipulated by provisions of the law.

Article 73
No commitment to pay a sum of money from the General Treasury shall be made without adherence to budget rules. If provisions of the budget cannot cover the demand, then a provision shall be made through a royal decree.

Article 74
Assets of the State may not be sold, rented or disposed of unless so authorised by the law.

Article 75
Laws shall specify provisions for currency, banks, standards, measures and weights.

Article 76
The law shall set the fiscal year for the State. The budget shall be announced according to a Royal Decree. It shall specify assessed amounts of revenue and expenditure one month ahead of the coming fiscal year. If the budget cannot be issued due to compelling reasons before the beginning of the new fiscal year, the budget of the previous year shall remain in force until the new budget can be issued.

Article 77
The competent department shall prepare the closing account of the State for the past year and forward it to the Prime Minister.

Article 78
Budgets and the closing of accounts of departments which have corporate rights, shall be subject to the same procedures which are applicable to the State's budget and closing accounts.

Chapter Eight

Institutions of Audit

Article 79
All revenues and expenditures of the State, as well as movable and fixed assets, shall be subsequently audited to ensure proper use and management. An annual report to this effect shall be forwarded to the Prime Minister. The law shall specify details of the competent auditing institution, together with its affiliations and areas of authority.

Article 80
Governmental institutions shall also be audited to ensure proper administrative performance and implementation of laws. Financial and administrative violations shall be investigated. An annual report shall be forwarded to the Prime Minister. The law shall specify details of the competent institution in charge, together with its affiliations and areas of authority.

Chapter Nine

General Principles

Article 81
With regard to treaties and agreements, the application of this Law shall not violate commitments of the Kingdom of Saudi Arabia towards other states, international organisations and bodies.

Article 82
No provision of this Law whatsoever may be suspended except on a temporary basis, such as in wartime or during the declaration of state of emergency. Such a suspension shall be in accordance with the terms of the law and may not violate Article 7.

Article 83
No amendment to this law shall be made, except in the same manner as it was promulgated.

Appendix IV

In the name of God, the Most Compassionate, the Most Merciful,

No. A/13
Date: 3/3/1414H

With the help of God, we, Fahd Bin Abd - al Aziz Al-Su'ud, Monarch of the Kingdom of Saudi Arabia, after reviewing the Basic Law of Government, issued by Royal Decree No. A/90, dated 27/8/1412H, having reviewed Majlis Ash Shura Law issued by Royal Decree No. 1, dated 27/8/1412H, and having reviewed the Royal Decree No. M/23, dated 26/8/1412H, we, Fahd bin Abd - al Aziz Al-Su'ud, King of the Saudi Arabia, have decreed the following:

1. the promulgation of the Law of the Council of Ministers as in the attached text,

2. That this law supersedes Council of Ministers Law issued by a Royal Decree NO. 38, dated 22/10/1377H, and its amendments,

3. That all regulations, orders and decrees in force shall remain valid when this Council of Ministers Law comes into force until they are amended to conform with it,

4. That this decree shall be published in the Official Gazette and shall come into force ninety (90) days after the formation of Majlis Ash Shura, as stipulated in the first Royal Decree concerning it.

The General Principles of the Council of Ministers Law

Article 1
The Council of Ministers is a regulatory authority and the King is the Prime Minister.

Article 2
The city of Riyadh is the seat of the Council of Ministers. Meetings may also be held in some other location in the Kingdom.

Article 3
It is stipulated that every member of the Council of Ministers shall be:
a. A Saudi national by birth and descent,
b. A person well-known for righteousness and capability,
c. Of good conduct and reputation, not previously convicted for a crime of immorality or dishonour.

Article 4
Prior to the assumption of their duties, the Ministers shall take the following oath before the King:
"I swear by God Almighty to be loyal to my religion, then to my King and country. I swear not to reveal any of the State's secrets, to protect its interests and laws, and to perform my duties with sincerity, integrity and fairness."

Article 5
The office of minister may not be combined with any other government post, unless the need for such an exception arises and the Prime Minister approves it.

Article 6
A cabinet minister may not buy, lease, rent directly or through a proxy, or by public auction, any of the properties of the State. A minister also may not sell or offer for rent any of his properties to the government. A minister may not engage in any commercial or financial enterprises. A minister also may not accept board membership in any firm.

Article 7
The Council of Ministers meetings are presided over by the King, who is the Prime Minister, or by a deputy of the Prime Minister. The resolutions of the Council of Ministers become final after the King's approval.

Article 8
Cabinet ministers are appointed, relieved of their duties and their resignation accepted by Royal decree. Their duties are determined in accordance with Article 57 and 58 of the Basic Law of the Government.

The By-laws of the Council of Ministers shall stipulate their rights.

Article 9
The fixed term of the Council of Ministers shall be four years, during which a new council may be formed by Royal Decree. If the term expires before the formation of the new council, the previous council shall remain active until the new council is formed.

Article 10
A minister is the ultimate authority in running the affairs of his ministry, and the carries out his duties in accordance with ruling of this law as well as other laws and regulations.

Article 11
a.   Only a minister shall deputise for another minister in the Council of Ministers and in accordance with a decree issued by the Prime Minister.
b.   A deputy minister shall assume the responsibilities of the Minister in the latter's absence.

The Formation of the Council of Ministers

Article 12
The Council of Ministers shall be composed of:
a.   A Prime Minister,
b.   Deputy Prime Ministers,
c.   Ministers with Portfolios,
d.   Ministers of State appointed as members of the Council of Ministers by Royal Decree,
e.   Counsellor of the King, appointed members of the Council of Ministers by Royal Decree.

Article 13

The right to attend meetings of the Council of Ministers shall be an exclusive right of its ministers and the Secretary General of the Council of Ministers. At the request of the Prime Minister, or a minister of the Council, and with the approval of the Prime Minister, a state official or an expert shall be permitted to attend the meetings of the Council of Ministers to present information and explanations. The right to vote belongs exclusively to the ministers.

Article 14

Any meeting held by the Council of Ministers shall not be considered official without a quorum of at least two-third of its members. Resolutions shall not be considered official without majority approval. In case of a tie, the Prime Minister shall cast the deciding vote. In exceptional cases, meetings of the Council of Ministers may be considered official with half of the members in attendance. In such cases, resolutions shall not be considered official without the approval of at least two-thirds of the members in attendance. Such exceptional cases are decided by the Prime Minister.

Article 15

The Council of Ministers shall not pass a resolution relevant to a ministry in the absence of the concerned minister or whoever deputises for him unless it is absolutely necessary.

Article 16

The deliberations of the Council of Ministers are confidential. Resolutions are public except those deemed classified in accordance with a resolution by the Council of Ministers.

Article 17

Ministers of the Council shall be tried for violations committed in carrying out official business in accordance with a special law which specifies the violations, the procedures for prosecution and trial and the formation of courts.

Article 18

The Council of Ministers shall form committees from its members or from others, to study an issue on the agenda of the Council and prepare a special report about it. The By-laws of the Council shall specify the number of committees and the rules of procedure.

The Functions of the Council of Ministers

Article 19

While deferring to provisions of the Basic Law of Government and the Shura Council Law, the cabinet shall draw up the internal, external, financial, economic, educational and defence policies as well as general affairs of the State and shall supervise their implementation. It shall also review the resolutions of the Shura Council. It has the executive power and is the final authority in financial and administrative affairs of all ministries and other government institutions.

Regulatory Affairs

Article 20

While deferring to Majlis Ash-Shura Law, laws, treaties, international agreements and 'concessions' shall be issued and amended by Royal Decrees after deliberations by the Council of Ministers.

Article 21

The Council shall study draft laws and regulations on the agenda and vote on them chapter by chapter and then as a whole in accordance with the By-laws of the Council.

Article 22

Every minister may propose a draft law or regulation related to work of his ministry. Every member of the Council of Ministers may propose what he deems worth of discussion in the Council of Ministers' meetings after the approval of the Prime Minister.

Article 23

All laws shall be published in the *Official Gazette* and shall be put into force from the date of its publication unless it is stipulated otherwise.

Executive Affairs

Article 24

The Council, being the ultimate executive authority, shall have full jurisdiction over all executive and management affairs. The following shall be included in its executive jurisdiction:

1. Monitoring the implementation of regulations, by-laws and resolutions.
2. Creating and ranging public institutions.
3. Following up on the implementation of the general for development.
4. Forming committees for the oversight of the ministries and other governmental agencies conduct of business. Those committees may also investigate any given case. The committees shall submit the findings of their investigations within a set time to the Council and the Council shall consider these findings. It shall have the right to form committees of inquiry accordingly to make a final conclusion taking into consideration the regulations and stipulations of the By-laws.

Financial Affairs

Article 25

The government shall not contract a loan without the approval of the Council of Ministers and the issue of a Royal Decree so referring.

Article 26

The Council of Ministers shall examine the state budget, vote on each of its chapters. It is then promulgated by Royal Decree.

Article 27

Any supplement to the budget shall only be made by Royal Decree.

Article 28

The Minister of Finance and National Economy shall submit the closing account of the state from the previous fiscal year to the Prime Minister to be referred to the Council of Ministers for approval.

Presidency of the Council of Ministers

Article 29
The King, who is the Prime Minister, undertakes the guidance and supervision of the general policy of the State and secures guidance. co-ordination and co-operation among the various governmental agencies. He ensures harmony continuity and unity in all functions of the Council of Ministers. He supervises the Council of Ministers, the ministries and government agencies and monitors the implementation of regulations, by-laws and resolutions.

All ministries and other governmental agencies shall submit, within ninety (90) days from the beginning of each fiscal year, a financial report of what has been achieved in comparison with the stipulations of the general plan for development for the previous fiscal year. The report shall cover the difficulties of its implementation and proposals for improvement.

The Administrative Structure of the Council of Ministers

Article 30
The administrative structure of the Council of Ministers shall comprise:

1. The Office of the Prime Minister.
2. The General Secretariat of the Council of Ministers.
3. The Commission of Specialists.

The internal charter of the Council of Ministers shall specify the structures of these agencies, their jurisdictions and the manner of the performance of their duties.

Article 31
The By-laws of the Council of Ministers shall be issued by Royal Order.

Article 32
Modification of this law can only be made in the same manner of its issuance.

Appendix V

In the name of God, the Most Compassionate, the Most Merciful,

No. A/4
Dated 3/3/1414H.

With the help of God, we, Fahd Ibn Abd - al Aziz Al-Su'ud, Monarch of the Kingdom of Saudi Arabia, having reviewed Article 58 of the Basic Law of Government issued by Royal Order No. A/90 and dated 27/8/1412H, having reviewed the Law of the Ministers and Employees of the Highest Rank (Excellent Grade) issued by Royal Order No. M/10 dated 18/3/1391H, and in accordance with public interest, hereby order the following:

1.   The term of office for a minister or an employee of the highest rank (excellent grade) shall not exceed four years and his service shall terminate at the end of this period unless a royal order for extending it is issued.

2.   The term of office for whoever currently occupies the post of minister or a post of the highest rank (excellent grade) shall terminate two years after the issuance of this order unless a royal order for its extension is issued for a further period not to exceed two years. Unless a royal order for a further extension at the end of this tenure is issued according to item (1) of this order, the tenure shall terminate.

3.   The deputy premier and ministers shall implement this order of ours, each in his own jurisdiction.

The Law of the Provinces

(and the Royal Decrees Attached thereto)

The Custodian of the Two Holy Mosques, King Fahd Ibn Abd - al Aziz Al-Su'ud issued on Sunday 27th Shaban 1414H a Royal Decree embodying the Law of the Provinces.

The following is the text of the decree:

In the name of God, the Most Compassionate, the Most Merciful,

No. A92
Dated 27/08/1412H

With the help of God, we, Fahd Ibn Abd - al Aziz Al-Su'ud, Monarch of the Kingdom of Saudi Arabia, having taken into consideration the public interest and the wish to improve the standard of Government Institutions' performance and modernisation in various provinces, have ordered the following:
1.   The promulgation of the Law of the Provinces in the attached form,
2.   That this law shall come into force within a period not exceeding one year effective from the date of its publication,
3.   That this law shall be published in the Official Gazette.

In the Name of God, the Most Compassionate, the Most Merciful,

The Law of the Provinces

Article 1
The aim of this law is to improve the standard of the administrative work and the development in the provinces of the Kingdom. It is also aimed at maintaining security and order, and guaranteeing citizens' rights and freedom within the framework of the Shari'a.

Article 2
The provinces of the Kingdom and governmental seat of each province shall be formed according to a Royal Decree upon the recommendation of the Interior Minister.

Article 3
Administratively, every province shall consist of a number of governorates (of "Class A" or "Class B"), districts and centres (of "Cass A" or "Class B"). Full consideration shall be given to the factors of demography, geography, security, environment and communications. The organisation of a governorate shall be carried out according to a royal decree upon the recommendation of the

Interior Minister. Establishment of an affiliation of districts and centres shall take effect upon the Interior Minister's decision, as proposed by the emir of the province. (As amended by the Royal Decree A/21, dated 30/3/1414H).

Article 4
For each province, an emir with the rank of minister shall be appointed. A deputy at the highest (excellent) rank shall assist the emir and deputise for him during period for absence. The appointment and the relief of the emir and his deputy shall be made by Royal Decree upon the recommendation of the Minister of the Interior.

Article 5
The Emir of the Province shall be answerable to the Interior Minister.

Article 6
An emir and his deputy, prior to assuming their duties, shall take the following oath before the King:

> "In the name of God Almighty, I swear that I will be loyal to my religion then to my King and Country, will not reveal any of the State's secrets and will protect its interests and laws. I will perform my work in honesty, trust, sincerity and fairness."

Article 7
Every emir shall assure the administration of the region according to the general policy of the State in compliance with provisions of his Law and other laws and regulations. In particular, he is expected to do the following:

a.   Maintain security, order and stability, and take necessary measures in accordance with this law and other laws and regulations,
b.   Implement rulings of the courts upon acquiring their final dispositions,
c.   Guarantee human rights and freedom, refrain form any action which affects such rights and freedom except within the limits provided by the Shari'a and the law,
d.   Work for social and economic development and public works of the province,
e.   Work for the development and improvement of public services in the province,

f.   Administer governorates, districts and centres, and supervise governors, directors of districts and heads of centres, and ascertain their capabilities to perform assigned duties,

g.   Protect State property and assets, and prevent their usurpation,

h.   Supervise governmental institutions and their employees in the province and ensure proper performance of their work in honesty and loyalty with consideration of their affiliation with various ministries and service,

i.   Have direct contact with ministers and heads of agencies to discuss affairs of the province and improve the performance of affiliated institutions and to advise the Minister of the Interior accordingly,

j.   Submit annual reports to the Minister of the Interior on the efficiency of public services and other affairs of the province as defined by the executive provisions of this law. (As amended by the Royal Decree A/21, dated 30/3/1414H).

Article 8

An annual meeting, attended by emirs of provinces and presided over the Interior Minister, shall be held to discuss the affairs of the provinces. A report to this effect shall be forwarded to the Prime Minister by the Interior Minister.

Article 9

At least two meetings shall be held every year for governors and directors of districts to discuss the affairs of the province. The meeting shall be presided over by the emir, who shall submit a report to the Interior Minister. (As amended by the Royal Decree A/21, dated 30/3/1414H

Article 10

a.   Upon the recommendation of the Minister of the Interior, one deputy or more with a rank not less than Grade 14 shall be appointed for every province following a decision by the Council of Ministers.

b.   Every "Class A" governorate shall have a governor with a rank not less than Grade 14. Upon the recommendation of the Interior Minister, he shall be appointed by an order issued by the Prime Minster. The governorate shall have a deputy with a rank not less than Grade 12. He shall be appointed by a decision of the Minister of the Interior upon the recommendation of the emir of the province.

c.   Every "Class B" governorate shall have a governor with a rank not less than Grade 12. He shall be appointed by a decision of the Minister of the Interior upon the recommendation of the emir of the province.

d.   Every "Class A" district shall have a director with a rank of not less than Grade 8. He shall be appointed by a decision of the Minister of the Interior upon the recommendation of the governor.

e.   Every "Class B" district shall have a director with a rank of not less than Grade 5. He shall be appointed by decision of the emir of the province. (As amended by the Royal Decree A/21, dated 30/3/1414H)

Article 11
Emirs of provinces, governors of governorates and directors of districts shall reside in their work areas. They shall not be allowed to leave without permission from their direct superiors. (As amended by Royal Decree A/21, dated 30/3/1414H)

Article 12
The governors, directors of districts and heads of centers shall assume their responsibilities within their jurisdictions and within the assigned limits of their powers. (As amended by the Royal Decree A/21, dated 30/3/1414H)

Article 13
Governors shall manage their governorates within their limits of powers as provided in Article 7, excluding clauses (f), (i) and (j). They shall supervise the work of subordinate directors and heads of centres and ascertain their ability to perform their duties. They shall provide the Emir of the province with periodic reports about the efficiency of public services and other affairs of their governorates, as defined by the Executive Regulations of this law. (As amended by the Royal Decree A/21, dated 30/3/1414H)

Article 14
Every ministry or governmental organisation, having services in a province, shall appoint for its organs in the province a director with a rank not less than Grade 12. He shall be directly affiliated with the central institution and co-ordinate his work with the emir of the province.

Article 15
A council, called the Council of the Province, shall be established at every provincial seat.

Article 16
The council of a province shall be composed of:
a.   The emir of the province as chairman of the council,
b.   The deputy emir of the province as vice-chairman of the council,
c.   The deputy of the governmental seat,
d.   Head of governmental institutions in the province as specified by a resolution to be issued by the Prime Minister upon the recommendation of the Minister of the Interior.

e.   A minimum of ten men of knowledge, expertise and specialisation to be appointed from among the inhabitants by an order issued by the Prime Minister after their nomination by the emir of the province and the approval by the Minister of the Interior. Their terms of office shall be four years and shall be renewable. (Amended by Royal Decree A/21, dated 30/3/1414H)

Article 17
It is stipulated that every member of the Council shall be:

a.   A Saudi national by birth and descent,
b.   A person well-known for righteousness and capability,
c.   Not younger than 30 years of age,
d.   A resident of the province.

Article 18
A member shall be entitled to submit written proposals to the head of the provincial council on matters pertaining to the council's jurisdiction. Every proposal shall be listed by the chairman on the council's agenda for consideration.

Article 19
A member shall not attend discussions of the (provincial) council or its committees if the subject of discussion might concern his personal gain or might benefit individuals for whom his testimony is not acceptable, or individuals who have appointed him as guardian, proxy or representative.

Article 20
A Provincial Council member who wishes to resign shall submit his request to the Minister of the Interior through the emir of the province. His resignation shall not be considered valid until it is approved by the Prime Minister upon a proposal of the Minister of the Interior.

Article 21
In cases other than those mentioned in the Law, an appointed (provincial council) member may not be dismissed during the term of his membership without the Prime Minister's order after a proposal of the Minister of the Interior.

Article 22
When the place of any appointed (provincial council) member has become vacant for any reason, a successor shall be appointed within three months, effective from the beginning of vacancy. The term of the new member shall be

equal to the remaining period of his predecessor's term in accordance with Article 16, Clause (e) of this law.

Article 23
The council of province shall consider whatever might whatever might improve the standard of services in the province, particularly:

a. Defining needs of the province and proposing their inclusion in the State's Development Plan,

b. Defining useful projects and putting them in an order of priority, and proposing their endorsement in the annual budget of the State,

c. Studying urban plans for villages and towns of the province, and following up the implementation of all allocations to the province from the development plan and the budget,

d. Following up and co-ordinating the implementation of all allocations to the province from the development plan and the budget.

Article 24
The council of a provinces shall propose any work needed for the public interest of the population in the province, encourage citizens to participate in that work and submit the proposal to the Minister of the Interior.

Article 25
A provincial council is prohibited from considering any topic outside its jurisdiction as provided by terms of this law. Its decisions shall be null and void if its powers are misused. The Minister of the Interior shall issue a decision to this effect.

Article 26
The council of a province shall convene every three months in ordinary sessions upon invitation by its chairman. If he considers it necessary, the chairman is entitled to summon the council to an extraordinary session. The session shall include one or more meetings which are held upon a single summon. The session may not be adjourned until all issues on the agenda are taken into consideration and discussed.

Article 27
Those members who are mentioned in Article 16, Clauses (c) and (d) of this Law must attend meetings of the provincial council as part of their official duties. They should attend in person or appoint substitutes when they cannot attend. Regarding members mentioned in Clause (e) of the said Article, unexcused non-attendance at two successive sessions by a member shall be grounds for his dismissal from the council. In this case, he shall not be re-

appointed before two years have elapsed effective from the date of the decision for dismissal.

Article 28
Meetings of a provincial council shall not be official unless at least two-thirds of its members are present. Its resolutions shall be adopted by an absolute majority or votes of the council's members. In case of a tie vote, the chairman shall cast the deciding vote.

Article 29
A provincial council, in case of need, may form special committees to consider any topics within its powers. It may seek the assistance of experienced people and specialists. It may also invite others to attend the council's meetings and participate in discussions without having the right to vote.

Article 30
The Minister of the Interior may invite a council to convene under his chairmanship anywhere he deems suitable. He may chair any meeting he attends.

Article 31
A provincial council may not convene without an invitation its chairman or his deputy, or without an order issued by the Minister of the Interior.

Article 32
The chairman of a council shall submit a copy of the resolution to the Minister of the Interior.

Article 33
The chairman of a provincial council shall inform ministries and governmental services of any resolutions concerning them which are passed by the council.

Article 34
Ministries and governmental institutions shall take into consideration resolutions passed by a provincial council in accordance with provisions of Article 23, Clauses (a) and (b) of this law. If a ministry or a governmental institution does not agree to consider one of these resolutions, it shall explain the reasons to the provincial council. In case of dissatisfaction, the council shall refer the matter to the Minister of the Interior for reconsideration by the Prime Minister.

Article 35
Every ministry or institution with services in a province shall immediately inform the provincial council of projects which were decided upon in the budget for the province, together with its allocations from the development plan.

Article 36
Any minister or head of institution may seek the opinion of a provincial council on matters pertaining to his jurisdiction in the province. The council shall forward its opinion in this regard.

Article 37
The Council of Ministers, upon a proposal of the Minister of the Interior, shall set the remuneration of the chairman of a provincial council and its members, taking into account the cost of transportation and accommodation. (As amended by Royal Decree A/21, dated 30/3/1414H)

Article 38
A provincial council can be dissolved only on an order by the Prime Minister following the recommendation of the Minister of the Interior. New members shall be appointed within three months effective form the date of the dissolution. During the period, members mentioned in Article 16, Clauses (c) and (d) of this law, shall perform the duties of the council under chairmanship of the emir of the province.

Article 39
A secretariat for a provincial council shall be set up at the governmental seat of the province to prepare its agenda, send timely invitations, record discussions carried out during the sessions, count votes, prepare the minutes of sessions, draft decisions and perform necessary work for the monitoring of the council's session and the registration of all decisions.

Article 40
The Minister of the Interior shall issue the necessary regulations to implement this law.